Also by Alix Kates Shulman

NOVELS

In Every Woman's Life . . .
On the Stroll
Burning Questions
Memoirs of an Ex–Prom Queen

NONFICTION

A Good Enough Daughter: A Memoir
Drinking the Rain: A Memoir
Red Emma Speaks: An Emma Goldman Reader
To the Barricades: The Anarchist Life of Emma Goldman

FOR CHILDREN

Finders Keepers
Awake or Asleep
Bosley on Number Nine

To Love What Is

To Love What Is

A MARRIAGE TRANSFORMED

Alix Kates Shulman

FARRAR, STRAUS AND GIROUX

NEW YORK

Farrar, Straus and Giroux
18 West 18th Street, New York 10011

Copyright © 2008 by Alix Kates Shulman
All rights reserved
Distributed in Canada by Douglas & McIntyre Ltd.
Printed in the United States of America
First edition, 2008

Grateful acknowledgment is made to Harcourt, Inc., for permission to reprint
"Could Have," by Wislawa Szymborska.

Library of Congress Cataloging-in-Publication Data
Shulman, Alix Kates.
    To love what is : a marriage transformed / Alix Kates Shulman. — 1st ed.
    p.   cm.
    ISBN-13: 978-0-374-27815-1 (hardcover : alk. paper)
    ISBN-10: 0-374-27815-6 (hardcover : alk. paper)
    1. York, Scott—Mental health.   2. Brain damage—Patients—United
States—Biography.   I. Title.

RC387.5.S38 2008
617.4'81044092—dc22
[B]

                                                            2008021504

Designed by Jonathan D. Lippincott

www.fsgbooks.com

1   3   5   7   9   10   8   6   4   2

Certain names and identifying details have been changed
in the interest of privacy.

To my darling

So you're here? Still dizzy from another dodge, close shave,
  reprieve?
One hole in the net and you slipped through?
I couldn't be more shocked or speechless.
Listen,
How your heart pounds inside me.
                    —Wislawa Szymborska, "Could Have"

            It's all life until death.
                    —Grace Paley

To Love What Is

The Accident

On a moonless summer night my husband fell nine feet from a sleeping loft to the floor and did not die.

He did not die, though he was seventy-five years old and the accident happened in a remote seaside cabin inaccessible by road, on a Maine coastal island that has no doctor on call, much less a hospital.

He did not die, though X-rays taken several hours later showed that he had broken most of his ribs and both feet; punctured both lungs, causing perilous internal bleeding; and suffered so many blood clots in his brain that each CAT scan of that precious organ resembled an elaborate filigree.

He did not die, though my neighbor's husband fell from a tree and died in a week, and my doctor's father fell from his roof and died in a day.

How did it happen, that near-fatal fall which he somehow survived? What mysterious combination of mistakes and miracles? He can't remember it, and I, no matter how indelibly the details of that night are branded on my mind, still can't fathom it.

Like everyone over a certain age, I sensed that some dreadful thing was coming, the more ominous for not knowing what form it would take or when it would come or whether, when it finally arrived, I would rise to the challenge or succumb.

Every couple who stays together long enough has intimations that a catastrophe is waiting; it's right there in the wedding vows: *For better and for worse, in sickness and in health, till death do us part.* Having taken the oath, however cavalierly, you know that unless you separate, one of you is going to wind up taking care of the other, or one of you is going to wind up surviving the other. But which one it will be, when it will happen, how long it will last, and at what cost is unknown, though the odds predict that *she* will take care of *him*, then *he* will die, leaving *her* alone. But like a curse in a fairy tale, you don't really believe it's coming; you try to ignore it until it's upon you. In the enchantment of life, you forget.

Middle of the night, July 22, 2004. Many hours earlier, we'd left the great island of Manhattan for the small island of Long in Casco Bay, Maine, where we have a summer place. In two backpacks and a wheeled suitcase we'd lugged some basic supplies and everything we'd need for a couple of months of work: I, my laptop and a draft of a short novel to polish; Scott, plans for a new set of sculptures.

After an all-day bus ride from Manhattan to Boston and from Boston on to Portland, then an hour's ferry ride to the island, and, with our gear on our backs, a twenty-minute walk from where the road dead-ends at the ocean across a long beach to our house, we were pretty exhausted. Especially Scott, whose stamina has been waning for some time.

First mistake: to have taken the bus instead of flying.

By the time we reached the island, it was already late afternoon. Our nearest neighbors and closest island friends, Heather Lewis and Norm Fruchter, who, like us, live in New York in the winter, met our boat at the wharf and drove us in their truck to their house, which stands at the end of the road in front of the long beach that leads to our house. "Why don't you come back here and have dinner with us? You don't want to start cooking now," Heather said as we started across the beach with our gear. I couldn't figure out which would be more tiring: to rustle up a makeshift meal at home or walk back across the beach to Heather and Norm's. I said I'd call her later and let her know.

As Scott and I began to unpack and attend to the essential chores of opening our house for the summer—lighting the small propane fridge; priming the pump that draws water from the rain barrel beneath the deck; checking the propane-powered gas lamps; sweeping away the winter's mouse droppings; putting a roll of toilet paper out in the privy; and turning on the solar system I use to charge my laptop, printer, and cell phone in the separate studio Scott built for me—Heather's invitation became increasingly attractive. When we took a break from our labors I called her on my cell phone to say we'd be over in an hour, and after washing up and changing clothes, we walked back across the long beach to their house.

Second mistake: we should have stayed home, eaten bread and peanut butter, and gone straight to bed instead.

Eating Heather's delicious lasagna, catching up on island gossip, watching the sky take on the glow of sunset as we sipped wine (third mistake: allowing Scott half a glass, forbidden because it clashes with his meds)—I could have stayed for hours being cared for and amused at Heather's table; it was a perfect transition from the dense throb of Manhattan to our quiet island life. Over dessert, Scott leaned across to me and whispered that it was time to go home. "But we haven't finished our coffee," I said, and turned back to hear the end of a funny story.

Fourth mistake: I should have heeded the distress signal and left immediately.

At least another fifteen minutes passed before Scott, uncharacteristically, stood up, insisting that we leave at once, and I finally got the message.

We had barely started the trek across the beach toward

home when he began to complain of feeling weak and cold—
so cold that his teeth were actually chattering. I suggested that
we return to our friends' house, which unlike ours has all the
traditional amenities and comforts, and take them up on their
standing offer to spend the night. A fog was rolling in, and
though it was mid-July, there was a chill in the air. Why push
it? Ever since he'd survived an aortic aneurysm a dozen years
before, I'd felt protective of him, taking seriously each odd
symptom. But he refused to turn back, even after some urging,
so I took his arm and we pressed on.

Fifth mistake: I should have insisted that we turn back instead of crossing the long beach for the third time that day.

By the time we got home, it was dark. Instead of unpack-
ing, we decided to go to bed immediately. We left the house
and walked down the path past the outhouse, with its one-hole
privy, to the east-facing studio, where we often prefer to sleep
in order to wake up to the exhilarating sight of sunrise and surf
crashing on the rocks below. As is our habit, I preceded him up
the ladderlike stairs to the sleeping loft to light a gas lamp to il-
luminate his way up. When I had it lit, Scott locked the doors,
turned off the downstairs lamp, and followed me up. We got
into bed and talked a while before turning off the light. This
was always our pleasure, talking over the highlights of the day,
and tonight, having just arrived, admiring the studio Scott designed and built for me sixteen years before, with its steeply
pitched roof forming the high ceiling of the single room, its
asymmetrical fenestration, its lush mahogany floorboards of
irregular width, the gift of a boatbuilder friend, which we laid
and varnished together, and then our special game, identifying
animals and faces, as varied as the patterns in passing clouds, in
the knots of the pine boards that form the walls and ceiling.

Sixth mistake: knowing how tired he was, I should have
turned off the light at once and let him sleep.

When I finally closed my eyes, I fell instantly into a deep sleep. Too deep to notice Scott leaving the bed or remember his crying out, though I must have heard him, because—

Suddenly I'm sitting bolt upright in bed, flooded with adrenaline. In that black night it's almost too dark to see the empty place beside me, but I sense his absence. "Scott?" No answer. Louder: "Scott?" The studio where we sleep is a single room topped by the sleeping loft. If he doesn't answer, where can he be? "Scott? Scott!" Maybe he's gone off to the outhouse and can't hear me call. But inside me I know the catastrophe has come.

On top of a bluff that protrudes into the ocean from the edge of the rocky coast like a small peninsula—a shore formation called a nubble—the studio of pine and glass usually gets more than enough moonlight and starlight to see by; in a lightning storm the entire nubble is lit in every direction. But by this hour of the night the moon has set, and whatever ambient light might normally glow is obscured by a dense fog. Gas lamps take time to light—to find a match, strike it, then, with one hand hold it an exact distance beneath the lamp's delicate fiberglass mantle (any closer and the mantle would break), and with the other hand turn a difficult valve to allow the propane to flow into the lamp. Frantic for light, I instead grab the flashlight I keep next to the bed and shine it down over the low wall of the loft onto the floor below.

There he is, lying on the floor, curled up like a fetus. Naked and deathly still.

I dash down the steep stairs, shouting his name, then repeat it directly into his ear.

No response.

This can't be happening. I can't believe it's happening. Maybe it's not? All at once I recall the day, many years before, as the studio was being built, when I came inside to see Scott with hammer and nails high up on a tall ladder that leaned against the loft. Seconds later he and the ladder fell backward in a great arc to the floor, he landing on his back with the ladder on top of him. Although that fall was from almost the same height as tonight's fall, after a moment he got up and brushed himself off, with only a fright, a few bruises, and the next day a sore back.

This time he is silent and immobile.

More light! I set down the flashlight and light the nearest gas lamp, then crouch down beside him. "Scott!" I repeat, moving his shoulder—gently at first, then less gently. No response, nothing. Is he breathing? I hold my own breath to listen. I can't tell. I remember the mirror test, but there's no mirror.

His body isn't cold or gray or spurting blood—not that I can see, anyway—all good signs. But he doesn't respond. I refuse to believe—or even imagine the possibility—that he is dead.

My fault, my fault, my fault! For not waking up when he woke up. For not keeping a closer eye on him. For not nagging him to put a higher railing in the loft. For failing to insist that we spend the night at Heather and Norm's. For taking a bus from New York instead of a plane. For not seeing this coming. How could I have let this happen?

Somehow I manage to find my cell phone and call 911.

🐂

Eerily, over dinner that evening our neighbors had told us amusing gossip about infighting among the island's emergency rescue team, part of the Long Island Volunteer Fire Department. After the stories, it occurred to me to ask what number to call in an emergency. I was surprised to learn that it was now 911, rather than some ordinary island number, as it used to be.

Another eerie coincidence: in bed that night before we turned out the light, we talked about broken bones. I asked Scott, once a star athlete who in his youth had suffered his share of broken limbs, if there were nerves in bones to make them hurt. He speculated that what hurts is the adjacent tissue but not the bones themselves. The next day, recalling these coincidences under the terror of my guilt, irrationally I wonder if they might not be used as evidence to suggest that I pushed him over.

After I've described the accident to the 911 operator, he asks if Scott is unconscious.

"I don't know. He hasn't moved or spoken."

"Is he breathing?"

"I don't know," I admit again, feeling stupid.

Then suddenly Scott makes a sound—a senseless babble, like garbled underwater speech, stroke talk.

The first miracle: he's alive!

As I'm reporting this miraculous news, I hear him say, weakly, "Turn me on my back."

Not only alive but speaking!

Jubilantly I repeat his words into the phone and my worst fears vanish in the fog.

"Do not move him," orders the operator. "It will be dangerous to move him until a medic gets there and assesses him."

No sooner does one fear disappear than another one rushes in to fill the vacuum. Alive, coherent, but in what condition? And how will he be saved?

"Can you please tell me your address?"

Here is a problem. Our official post office address corresponds to a mailbox in front of Norm and Heather's house at the end of the nearest road, a twenty-minute walk across the beach from here. Useless for guiding anyone to us. I try to explain the difficulty, but it's futile. Why have I never prepared myself for this crucial question? Going back and forth with questions and answers, we waste precious moments, until I abandon the concept of address and tell the operator that we are on Long Island in Casco Bay, twenty minutes out beyond where the road to South Beach dead-ends, on a spit of land that juts out from the intersection of South Beach and Singing Sands Beach. The spit is called Andrews Nubble on the nautical charts. Assuming he'll send a helicopter to land on the beach, I imagine more minutes lost while he locates a nautical chart. "We have two structures," I warn, "the house and the studio. Three, if you count the small outhouse in between them. We're now in the studio, the farthest structure from Singing Sands Beach. It'll be the only one with lights on." I warn him about the steep, rickety stairs up from the beach, the rail-less deck, the pitch-black night.

"What's your husband's name?"

"Scott York."

"Age?"

"Seventy-five."

"Okay. Now, don't go away. I'm going to send out an emergency call. Whatever you do, don't move your husband until someone arrives. It may take me a while, so just hold on there. Don't hang up."

For two decades of summers I came to this island by myself, in love with solitude, my only connection with the outside world weekly phone calls from the island's single pay phone down near the dock or old-fashioned handwritten letters. The next miracle on that night of mistakes: the phone never once lost its signal, which is always chancy and quickly broken in this remote cabin. It's even something of a miracle that I have a cell phone at all, having bought it only after I began to worry about Scott alone in New York.

While I wait for rescue, I light the three downstairs gas

lamps, then run back upstairs, grab my watch (it's after two), and throw down a pillow and a sleeping bag to cover Scott with.

"Turn me on my back, please, it's killing me."

"I can't," I say, tucking the bag around him gingerly. "I'm not allowed to move you till a medic comes. You mustn't move. I'm so sorry." Over and over he pleads to be turned over. How can I go on refusing him? As I carefully slip the pillow beneath his head, I am seared by guilt for refusing to grant his wish— the first of many seemingly cruel refusals and tyrannical commands from me to him in the months to come.

Finally, the 911 operator comes back on the line to report that he's sent out the highest, most serious alarm, a Number 10.

I'm perplexed. Scott is talking okay, and I don't see any blood. "Why a Number 10?"

"An elderly man falls nine or ten feet and loses consciousness? That's a Number 10 if anything is."

Elderly? The word takes me by surprise. It applies to one's parents, not one's husband. Whenever our children have shown that they consider us old, we've balked or laughed. Scott, whom I fell for when he was twenty and I seventeen, is timeless to me, not elderly. Maybe that's why we fell in love a second time, after thirty-four years apart: in each other's eyes, we were still the (by then mythical) youths we'd been in 1950, the summer of our first romance.

❦

Science has firmly established that memory is unstable and unreliable, that whenever you summon up a recollection of the past you are liable to change it slightly until, with the passage of time, it may no longer represent what actually happened. Nevertheless, I can still see in my mind's eye, as clearly as if it were yesterday, the twenty-year-old Scott York, blond, blue-eyed, and fabulous, sitting halfway up in the biology amphitheater as I stood at the bottom surveying the room on my first day of college. From that moment on, I set my sights on him. Seventeen and newly sprung from Cleveland Heights High School, I was no longer subject to the rule by which Jews and gentiles were forbidden to date—a restriction so rigorously enforced that even at my thirty-fifth high-school reunion, held at a country club where the ballroom was divided by the dance floor into two separate wings, Jews occupied the tables on one side, gentiles those on the other, as Scott and I alone noticed.

He had long figured in my fantasies. When I was a freshman at Heights, he was a graduating senior—captain of the basketball team, president of his (gentile) fraternity, school vice president. At the games where I went to cheer my own (Jewish) boyfriend, it was Scott York I watched. At six feet, with thick blond hair, chiseled features, and muscular shoulders and thighs, he was a thing of beauty, despite the sweat staining his jersey or the occasional foul he inflicted with a well-placed elbow. His spectacular leaps to make the point, his perfect long shots from impossible distances, and his bone-risking dives to recover the ball made him the highest scorer, whose picture was often in the school paper and, during the championship play-offs, even in the Cleveland *Plain Dealer*. He had the speed and grace of an antelope—not only on the court but also on the dance floor, where he and his girlfriend Nancy were among the slow-dancing and jitterbugging couples people formed circles around to watch.

Now here he was in summer school, three years after having graduated from Heights, taking the same botany class I was taking—and a long summer ahead of us. The class would be meeting from nine till noon every weekday for the next six weeks; much could happen in six weeks' time. I had no illusion that he, who had left high school a semester after I entered, might remember me. Nevertheless, feeling predatory and bold, I walked up the steep steps and sat down beside him.

The biology building (now gone) was built at the beginning of the last century, with high ceilings, tall windows, dark wooden floors, and old-fashioned oak chairs that turned into desks when you swiveled up the heavy arm—an awkward maneuver. Scott graciously helped me unfold the arm of my chair. I put down my books and slipped my cardigan over the back of my seat before I flashed my most seductive smile and introduced myself. I couldn't tell if I'd made an impression on him until two days later, when, arriving in class after me, he scanned the faces in the hall and then made straight for the empty seat beside me.

Scott was a premed student at Duke, on a four-year basketball scholarship, spending his summer back home to earn money and get the extra science credits he needed to graduate the following year. Most of the jocks I knew went to one of the state colleges and studied business administration, not a hard major like premed. I was impressed. But then, I too had sobered up since I'd last seen him. Once a boy-crazy social butterfly, in my senior year I'd withdrawn into a cocoon of my own making and emerged a passionate seeker of knowledge who over the past year had begun to disdain the limitations of our one-track adolescent minds. As I became absorbed by books, my mind became two-track. Perhaps, after three years of college, Scott's was too? Over burgers and fries at the campus café I tried to draw him out, but as doggedly as I asked my questions, he was determined to deflect them, thus preserving his mystery.

Even if I'd succeeded, what can one know of another soul?—especially at seventeen, when the neural and social networks are more potential than secure. The assumptions we made about each other were based on the flimsiest preconceptions, which set us both up for some surprises. Not that I was surprised to find him an innocent when it came to girls—common enough in boys who thought of little but sports for most of their lives, faced with girls who thought of little but boys for most of theirs. A proud practitioner of feminine wiles as performed in Cleveland Heights, Ohio, I welcomed his social naïveté for the advantage it gave me against his three-year edge in years. But his reticence, his modesty, his lack of even a whiff of macho posturing surprised me in an athlete. In the jock culture of our high school, the athletes I knew were mostly so full of themselves that they thought they could get away with anything, from classroom cheating to rape; and though most of them never stooped that low, even the best were vain and self-important. Scott seemed different. Despite his uncommon good looks, he was shy, earnest, and humble, with a sweetness about him that puzzled me.

For his part, he was surprised by what he called my "braininess." He'd never before had a book-reading girlfriend. He knew his way around a microscope well enough—so well that he succeeded in getting me to see cells floating on a slide—but I doubted he'd read more than half a dozen unassigned books in his entire life. He questioned me about the books I loved, and sometimes he jotted down titles. (A half century later, packing up his studio, I came upon a small notebook of his from that summer, with a list of authors I'd suggested—Mencken, Emerson, Voltaire, and the debut fiction of Capote and Isherwood.) Evidently, I was as exotic to him as he was to me.

On the Friday of our second week, our class went on an expedition to Cleveland's Holden Arboretum. There, for the first time, Scott and I engineered a few minutes apart. A light rain was falling as we left the parking lot for the trail, allowing us to huddle arm in arm under a single umbrella. Walking slowly with the pretext of collecting leaves, we fell behind the class until we were alone, surrounded by nothing but woods. Scott stopped under the shelter of a tall Ohio buckeye, with its huge handlike leaves spread in benediction; then he took me in his arms and kissed me. Unlike other kisses I'd known, this one felt as chaste as it was ardent. There we stood in the rain, kissing, until Scott pulled away, murmuring an apology. For what? My age? Did he think me an innocent (like him)? Perhaps a virgin?

Time was slipping by; I had to disabuse him quickly, make him recognize me as not your ordinary freshman.

❦

A great pounding, and the studio door bursts open.

Another miracle—it's Greg Middleton, the island arborist. "Greg!" I cry giddily. What a relief that the first rescue worker to arrive is not some stranger dropping from a helicopter, but a friend. Never have I been gladder to see anyone. I want to throw myself at his feet, put our lives in his hands.

He sweeps a powerful torch around the studio, then rushes over to Scott and crouches down beside him. "How ya doin', buddy?" he asks softly. He moves away to report his arrival into a big boxy radio.

"How did you hear?" I ask.

"The radio woke me up. As soon as I heard the dispatcher say Singing Sands Beach, I knew it had to be you. I jumped into my boots and took off."

"You sleep with the radio on?"

"When I'm on duty I sure do." He looks up at the sleeping loft. "He fell from way up there? Wow! What happened?"

Before I can answer, there's more pounding on the door and

three more men explode into the room, breathless, wired, filling the small studio with their bristling male energy and the crackling static of their radios. From every corner of the island, one by one, the heroic Long Island Volunteer Fire and Rescue Team burst through the door, then report by radio to the fire chief. They include several lobstermen, a carpenter, the builder who put in our solar, the island gas man, a hospital orderly who commutes to Portland. Some I know, some I don't. The last to arrive is Tim Lambert, the EMT medic. Taking charge, Tim kneels down to Scott, while the rest of the men huddle around him in a closed circle that excludes me, and asks me for a list of Scott's medications.

Why have I never compiled such a list? (Nowadays I keep one in each of our wallets and all over our loft.) I get the pills, but before I begin to write, I see a stretcher being readied. Afraid of being left behind, I quickly snatch up Scott's things—his wallet, medicines, clothes, shoes, glasses—and, together with a flashlight and my cell phone, throw them into my still partially packed backpack. Everything is happening so fast! I'm barefoot when the men start out the door with Scott on the stretcher. Frantically I fumble to put on sneakers. Greg stays behind to help me close the studio and with his powerful torch guides me back across the decks, down the iffy stairs, and on across the narrow path from Singing Sands to the longer South Beach, where the hazards of high tide await us.

Usually the beach is wide and firm enough to run across, but at high tide it shrinks to a strip of wrack strewn with treacherous driftwood, rocks, rope, and plastic—too narrow for a stretcher and its bearers. Nevertheless—another miracle—somehow the men manage to carry the stretcher in relays across that long beach without stumbling, though it's almost impossible to see the ground for the soupy fog. I trot along at the rear, trying to keep up, afraid of being left back as superfluous or worse.

At last we reach the end of the beach, where the road begins in front of Heather and Norm's house, and the island's ambulance truck awaits us. I look up. Their windows are dark, the house is still. Can it really have been only a few hours since we sat on that porch and laughed through dinner, carefree and confident? I see through a scrim to that distant world where life proceeds by days and nights, not minute by terrifying minute; it occurs to me that we've left that calm, carefree world behind forever.

But there's no time to think. The men are already transferring Scott from the stretcher to a gurney and lifting him into the truck. Someone leads me to the truck's cab, where I can ride beside the driver. Someone else thrusts my bag onto my lap, and off we go, racing across the island through the fog, down to the dock where the fireboat from Portland, fitted out as an ambulance, awaits us. In the fog I can just make out Dickey Clarke, the fire chief—whose day job is to run the island dump—standing on the wharf directing the rescue with radio and bullhorn. Despite the hour, some of the island women have also turned out to lend support; Robin, who is part of the rescue team, wishes me luck as Scott is wheeled onto the boat.

Now we've pulled anchor and are heading out to sea. The island recedes, our friends are gone. Seeing it disappear, I feel a wave of overwhelming gratitude toward those heroic men and women who showed up in the middle of the night to save my husband. Without them, how will I be able to protect him from further harm?

Inside the truck's cabin, the gurney is secured to the floor. A medic claps an oxygen mask over Scott's mouth and nose. At last I can see his pale blue eyes, study that handsome face. It's changed; it radiates less light. He's trying to say something, but behind the mask his words are too muffled to make out. All I can do is stroke his forehead and hands and try to reassure him that things are under control and that he'll be okay.

"How long before we get to Portland?" I ask the medic.

"Maybe twenty, twenty-five minutes," he says of a trip that by ferry would normally take forty-five minutes, including stops. I check my watch. Almost 4:00 a.m.—two hours since the universe flipped over. Silently I urge the boat to go still faster.

※

More than half a century before, at the end of our second week of summer school, Scott finally took me out on a genuine date. He picked me up in his secondhand blue Ford convertible and drove us to the Sea Fare Lounge, a smoky cocktail bar with live piano music and leather banquettes, at the edge of Cleveland Heights, halfway down the long hill to the city—more sophisticated than the high-school hangouts I was used to. On a platform just inside the entrance, a gaunt brunette, cigarette dangling from her lips, played show tunes on a baby grand and nodded to Scott as we entered. When he told me she was a classmate of his, I felt intimidated and jealous. Could she be the reason we'd come here?

We slid into a booth and ordered shrimp cocktails and martinis. Though Scott sat with his back to the pianist, giving me his full attention, I bridled when she dedicated a song to him. That a Heights High girl could or would have a job playing music in a cocktail bar was unimaginable to me. Though I was prettier, she was at least twenty, and far more accomplished. What cards did I have to play?

("Don't kid yourself, you had plenty of cards," Scott tells me decades later when I read him this passage off my computer screen.)

After my second martini I played the sex card, my one trump, and lightheartedly challenged him to find us a bed where we could make love. No backseats for us! I said it with enough flippant bravado that he could dismiss it as a joke if he wanted to, though I'd already tried to make clear that I disdained prudery and considered myself not bound by Heights High conventions.

He said nothing, just leaned over to light my cigarette—a Chesterfield, my mother's brand—though he himself, like my upright father, was not a smoker. Was he shocked by my invitation? When he took me home and chastely kissed me good night on the front porch, it was as if he had not heard my challenge. So I was surprised when, on our next Saturday night date, instead of taking me dancing or home, he headed across the bridge spanning the Cuyahoga River to Cleveland's West Side, where neither of us knew a soul, and turned into the entrance drive of a motel.

A motel! In the movies, motels were where seductive fallen women and doomed married lovers begin their plunge.

"Wait here," he said, getting out of the car and heading toward the office.

Embarrassment and exhilaration battled inside me as I waited. Motel sex was supposed to be sordid, base, degrading. But I was relieved that *it* was finally going to happen and ecstatic that despite his inhibiting shyness, gentleman that he was, he had accepted my dare. Seeing him return to the car waving a room key, my admiration for him soared.

In 1984, when he suddenly reappeared in my life after a thirty-four-year hiatus, Scott amazed me by recalling the name and address of the motel, complete with our room number (26). What I remembered was that for all my swagger, we spent a good half hour sitting on the bed talking before taking off our clothes. As we try now, in 2005, to reconstruct our early courtship, the passage of more than half a century has left only a few images undimmed and undiminished. For me, the layout of the room, the smell of woolen blankets even in summer, the Big Ben clock ticking on the night table, and, most vividly, his hard, smooth biceps pressed against my cheek while we made love, and afterward the bedsheets soaked with his sweat ("It was summer, what do you expect?" he protests defensively when I read him this passage); for him, the shock of seeing my black pubic triangle as I emerged naked from the bathroom. When I question him and probe for more, nothing comes; he can't remember anything but what he's told me already. It can't be only a result of his brain injury, because I, who once prided myself on my memory for detail, retain of that faraway time only the few images I've recorded here from which to infer what our affair meant to me, to us, what really happened.

That summer, though we did manage several quick couplings in the car, we never returned to the motel or made love in a bed again. Nor did we speak of the sex we shared, even though when the botany course ended, we both registered for zoology, giving us six more weeks of class together, plus weekend afternoons in my parents' garage dissecting the frog we stole from the lab in order to study for the final, and our regular Saturday nights. What kept us from going back again? Embarrassment? The risk of being caught? The expense? Perhaps it was my unspoken understanding that although the romance was of a high order, the sex, like most sex between the inexperienced, was not worth the risks. Like any 1950 Heights High girl, I feared being carried away and losing control, which could lead, in those pre-pill years, to pregnancy, exposure, ruin. As for him, if he'd felt apologetic for merely kissing me, how much more so must he have felt over having sex with me. Having demonstrated to each other our daring and audacity, perhaps prudence induced us to quit while we were ahead.

TWO

The Hospital

In the emergency room of Maine Medical Center, Scott's gurney disappears through windowless double doors and I am directed into a small, fluorescent-lit waiting room opposite, equipped with phones, pens and pads, and boxes of tissues. At last I am free to cry. Once the tears begin to fall, I can't stop them. Too distracted to sit, I pace up and down the small room, wadding up tissues. Though I had made a fetish of solitude, priding myself on my ability to flourish for months at a time alone on the nubble without phone, power, or companion, I have never felt as alone and afraid as I feel now.

At last Dr. Cushing enters the room and closes the door behind him. In a strong Boston accent reminiscent of JFK's, he introduces himself as head of the trauma unit. He reports that after preliminary examination, it seems that Scott has lost a great deal of blood through internal bleeding, but in his opinion he has a good chance of surviving.

This news is so shocking that I collapse into a chair. From the time the rescue team arrived, I had never faced the possibility that he might not survive. "Are you telling me he could die?"

"At this point we can't really say. But we're going to do our best to pull him through."

The bottom drops out. I feel nauseated and faint. As I hear

the details of Scott's dire condition—his punctured lungs, broken bones, and bleeding brain—the gravity of a Number 10 finally begins to register.

Maybe this Dr. Cushing, who despite his authoritative manner can't be much over forty, doesn't know what he's talking about.

"Does Mr. York have any advance directives—living will, health-care proxy, power of attorney?" he asks. I nod. "Good," he says approvingly, standing up. "You can see him now."

He leads me out of the little room through the double doors into the trauma center, where Scott lies on a gurney fully alert, talking to the nurses. "Hi, darling," he says to me, as if I've just come in from shopping.

Dr. Cushing approaches him. With everyone in the room as witness—several doctors, four or five nurses, and other staff—he says, "Mr. York. The CAT scans indicate that you have blood clots on your brain. We don't know the extent of the damage, but if it seems that you wouldn't be able to resume an independent life, would you want us to try to keep you alive?"

Scott reflects only a moment before saying, "No, I don't think so." And then firmly: "No."

These are the words I will play over and over in my mind in the months and years to come: *If it seems that you wouldn't be able to resume an independent life, would you want us to try to keep you alive?* And the unequivocal answer: *No, I don't think so. No.*

But at the time, what I feel is pride in this man, so principled that he'll stick to his guns even in the face of death.

The doctor nods. "All right then," he says, turning to the others. "Let's get him intubated."

❧

When I first met him, Scott lived with his parents in one half of a rented side-by-side house on an old street in a middle-class

Cleveland suburb, where, compared with their neighbors, most of whom owned their own homes, the Yorks were the working poor. Scott's mother's family had been farmers and his father's family steelworkers who raised their sons up into Ohio's middle class by helping them become doctors and dentists. But Scott's father, a dentist, suffered from such severe chronic migraines that his practice dwindled away. He searched everywhere for an explanation and a cure, consulting doctors as far away as Montreal, where the famous neurosurgeon Wilder Penfield drilled a hole in his skull ("to relieve the pressure"), which he then repaired with a permanent steel plate, to no avail. While Scott was a boy, his father, in his agony, became addicted to the painkiller Seconol, a powerful barbiturate, for which he as a dentist was able to write his own prescriptions. He sent Scott, an only child, off to various pharmacies to have them filled. Several times a day he injected Seconal into his veins, but even so, during a migraine the slightest sound was so painful to him that he sometimes banished his wife and son from their house until it passed, sending them off to stay with relatives. Before his affliction he'd been a devoted father, coaching the neighborhood boys in baseball, football, and basketball from the time Scott was six, forming them into teams for which Scott's mother sewed uniforms. While her husband's practice flourished, she ran the office, making the appointments and keeping the books, but after he became addicted and the practice shrank, it was she who supported the family—during the Depression as a switchboard operator, then, during World War II, as a parts inspector in an airplane factory, where she continued to work, inspecting jet engine rotor blades, for most of her life, eventually earning five-, ten-, and fifteen-year "veteran employee" pins, bejeweled with a tiny pearl, ruby, and diamond, respectively.

I met his mother, Myrtle, and his father, Russell, only once, briefly. The one Saturday Scott drove me to his house, he intro-

duced me to them quickly before hurrying me upstairs to his
banner-decorated room. I remember their Norman Rockwell
looks, Russell slim and craggy, Myrtle pleasant and plain in a
flowered housedress. Not a book was visible anywhere, unlike
my parents' house, which was filled with them. By the 1980s,
when Scott and I reconnected, both his parents were dead. His
father died in his fifties of smoke inhalation after setting their
house on fire by falling asleep with a lit cigarette; his mother
died in her sixties from a stroke, after suffering for years from
multiple sclerosis.

Scott himself started working in the fourth grade—after
school, on weekends, and during the summers—delivering
newspapers, scraping dishes in his grade-school cafeteria in exchange for lunch, shoveling snow and mopping kitchen floors
in various schools for the Cleveland Heights Board of Ed., sell-
ing magazines door-to-door, setting pins in the bowling alley,
working in the locker room at Cumberland Pool, coaching little kids at basketball, as a soda jerk, playing records at fraternity
dances, as an iceman transporting three-hundred-pound blocks
of ice on his shoulders up apartment-house stairs, and one
summer conveying machine parts on the floor of the very factory where his mother worked. All the money he ever had, he
earned himself. He went to Duke, in North Carolina, on a basketball scholarship, without which he might not have gone to
college at all. The scholarship paid for his tuition and a bed
over the gym in a long dormitory reserved for athletes, but, unlike nowadays, nothing more. From his freshman year on, he
played varsity and also took every job he could snag—as a dish-
washer in the cafeteria in exchange for board, as an orderly in
the Duke hospital, as a companion to the mentally ill, as a ven-
dor at the football games—and by joining the navy ROTC he
exchanged three years of navy service after graduation for the
extra stipend it offered, which he sent home to help support his
parents.

He was proud of his knack for finding work and was always on the lookout for more. I was mildly shocked, both by the job résumé itself and his evident pride in it, which made him all the more mysterious. My own Saturday job throughout high school at a local dress shop and the occasional summer job I took for pocket money, which I usually blew on milk shakes and clothes, would not have affected my living standard, since it was always understood that my parents would support me through college, expecting me to work at nothing but my studies. The sheltered daughter of a lawyer turned labor arbitrator and a teacher turned homemaker, I didn't appreciate the contortions it took for Scott to fit hours of varsity practice, ROTC training, and unskilled work into every spare moment between classes while still managing to keep up his grades. That he was a serious boy whose eager labors revealed unusual ambition, tenacity, and discipline failed to register. It was enough for a summer fling that I found him handsome, sexy, sweet, attentive, and different

We both knew from the start that our lives, barely beginning, were headed off in different directions, and that come autumn, when he packed up to leave for Duke, our romance would end. Creatures of Heights High, we never even introduced each other to our friends, keeping our affair private by default. Still, on our last date before he left Cleveland, I promised to write to him, and he said he'd call me when he came home for Christmas.

❦

It's still night. I'm in another waiting room, larger but also windowless, down the hall from the ICU, when a young, dark-haired woman, tall and vivacious, who introduces herself as Scott's nurse, takes me aside and asks in a low voice if I've started summoning the family yet.

Summoning the family! "Are you trying to tell me that he's about to die?"

"No, but you never know what's going to happen. Better to notify the family sooner rather than later, give them a chance to come."

I reel from her blow as if she's hit me in the stomach. At that moment I can't face telling anyone what's happened. To speak of it, as she wishes, would be to set it in stone. First I need to know he's recovering. "They all live far away from here, in New York City or Boston. They can't just drop everything and come to Portland."

"Shouldn't that be up to them? You wouldn't forgive yourself if something happened and you hadn't given them the option."

If Scott were to die, as she's so wantonly implying, then neglecting to notify the family in advance would not be at the top of my list of failings for which I would never forgive myself. Why is this stranger being so cruel? She is the one I won't forgive.

"I didn't give my family the chance when my father had his heart attack, and then he died," she confides. "I've never forgiven myself. I'm trying to spare you that. Anyway, you're a wreck," she says, observing my unceasing tears. "You shouldn't be alone now. You need someone with you."

What does she know about me or my needs?

"You should get yourself something to eat. You have to take care of yourself, you'll need your strength. You can't use a cell phone on this floor, but you can make calls from the cafeteria. It's straight down that hallway, then turn left at the exit sign."

In the grip of powerful emotions that interfere with my ability to think, I cannot but submit to her will. Outside the cafeteria windows, dawn is beginning to color the bottom of the sky with yellow and streaks of vivid rosy green. After the windowless waiting rooms where I've spent the night, it's a shock to see the ordinary, multicolored world, where people, mostly hospital workers, freely come and go to sip coffee and chat at long tables. Yesterday I was part of it; now I'm an alien with no visa and no prospects.

When I'm finally allowed into Scott's room in the ICU, he's out like a zombie and riddled with tubes. A breathing tube snakes from the computerized respirator down his windpipe to his lungs. A feeding tube runs through his nose down his throat to his stomach. From each side, chest tubes drain the fluid and air from the area around his lungs into large bloody containers on the floor beside the bed. An IV line enters an artery, a catheter in his penis drains his bladder, and cuffs that automatically inflate every few seconds to stimulate circulation encircle his ankles and lower calves. My darling who so recently expressed a tough, rational decision about his future has been replaced by someone completely inaccessible.

I'm stunned by his grotesque transformation not eight hours after his fall. His face is so swollen that it's hard to see where his jaw ends and his neck begins. His hands and feet are twice their normal size. The electronic scale attached to his bed registers the weight of this lean man at an astonishing two hundred pounds.

Lying there bloated and barely breathing, he reminds me of the sick pilot whale that beached itself on South Beach in full view of my house. No ICUs or respirators to help dying sea mammals breathe when they are too weak to surface in the water. Instead, there was another kind of "intervention." A special vet administered a lethal injection. In the autopsy that followed, eleven "rescue" workers in rubber boots spread out along the whale's entire length and, with a great heave, rolled him over so that his underside when slit open would drain to the sea via channels they dug in the sand. At dead low tide, the vet made the primary incision, using what looked like a long kitchen knife as scalpel. Two-foot sections of skin and blubber were peeled back to reveal the extravagantly magnified mammalian interior, so like ours. Small samples of skin, muscle, blood, urine, bile, intestine, lymph nodes, spleen, testes, bone, and every major organ, including—after the skull was opened with hacksaw and crowbar—brain, were preserved in formaldehyde for future study. Six hours after the first incision, when the rising tide reached the body, staining the water red, a lobster boat towed the whale's remains to a solitary burial at sea.

"It's going to be a very bumpy road before your husband is in the clear," warns Dr. Cushing gravely. "We're just going to have to wait and see what happens."

My best friend, Linda, sits beside me, squeezing my hand. When I'd called her in New York at 6:00 a.m. from the hospital cafeteria, she'd said, "I'm taking the first flight to Portland. Don't even bother trying to talk me out of it. I'm coming, period!"—and here she is with me, at the long counter in the nurses' station, where Dr. Cushing is showing us CAT scans of Scott's brain on a computer screen.

"See these dark spots? They're blood clots, subdural hematomas. We'll be watching the swelling very closely for the next seventy-two hours. After that, it could be eight months or a year or even more before we know the extent of the injury."

Eight months! Linda gasps. I'm too stunned to gasp.

We lie talking on a mattress in the carpeted studio of Linda's Portland friend Jane, who is traveling in Asia. The room is spacious and serene, decorated with large Tibetan wall hangings that glitter with gold. I stare at the elaborate silk tonkas, but they barely register; my focus is on my only goal in life: to keep Scott alive.

The next morning and every morning after, as soon as I'm dressed, I leave Linda asleep and walk to the hospital through empty streets. Once I arrive in Scott's room, at 8:00 a.m., I stay with him till 6:00 or 7:00 p.m., when I walk back to Jane's. I know I ought to use my walking time to figure out what to do, but I can't think, except about the past—about how far we've come, Scott and I, and what a miracle it is that we wound up together after thirty-four years apart.

Not that we ever forgot about each other. His name is scattered through my notebooks of the 1970s without explication or explanatory gloss: *Scott York*, nothing more—the associations, characterizations, and feelings it evoked seemingly self-evident. The first time I went to Cleveland to visit him after he'd finally reappeared in my life in 1984, something prompted me to take him up to the attic of my parents' house, which they had bought in the 1950s, soon after I'd moved to New York. I didn't know exactly what I'd find up there, but I must have had some inkling, because when I reached into the steamer trunk my mother had filled with my belongings when they moved, I pulled out a large matted photo of him in his white ensign's uniform and, buried further down, his blue satin varsity warm-up jacket, which neither of us remembered his having given me, with his number, 22, and D-U-K-E appliquéd in white letters.

Dr. Cushing has warned that the path to recovery will be bumpy—but like a mine-strewn road? I rejoice over each sign of progress, and though I reel with every setback, I don't collapse.

One morning I arrive to find Scott's right arm swollen to the size of a small tree trunk and covered from fingers to elbow with huge blisters. His fingers are like sausages and his hand is blue. At first no one knows why; then someone figures out that it's a chemical burn from a botched injection of CAT-scan dye into a vein. Before the Burn Unit is summoned, a nurse mentions the prospect of amputation. Another day there's fluid in a lung, which they'll have to drain by needle. Now it's internal bleeding, requiring more transfusions. Now one infection, detected in the white blood count, now another—but where each originates no one knows. The worst is his agitation, which leads him to pull out the feeding tube, the breathing tube, the IV line. The stronger he grows, the more of a threat he becomes to his own survival. After a record five agitated nights with no sleep at all, they tie his hands with restraints to keep him from pulling out his tubes again and only untie them in the daytime when I'm there to watch him every second. They shoot him with an antianxiety drug, then an antipsychotic. To enable him to sleep, they keep upping the dosages, but as often happens in the ICU, where artificial lights obliterate night and day, instead of returning to normal sleep patterns, he's out cold all day, day after day, sleeping like a junkie, and still no rest at night. For fear of what might have transpired in my absence, I'm often afraid to enter his room in the morning.

Though the breathing tube blocks his larynx and prevents his speaking, soon he is able to squeeze my hand, point, gesture, smile, shake or nod his head, and mouth words that I can't understand. Like a folie à deux, Linda and I egg each other on, imposing increasingly fanciful interpretations on his every wordless grimace or gesture. After we decorate his walls with art posters from the Portland Art Museum, we presume to read his pleasure. We never consider that he might be out of his mind, only that he can't speak it. When he blows me kisses as I leave, he seems himself.

But since he can't talk, who knows what he really thinks or feels? The truth is, I've never known what goes on in his head, even when he was in perfect health and we'd lived together for years. How often did I used to ask him, in the way of lovers, "What are you thinking?" without receiving any better answer than "Nothing," or "I was wondering what *you* were thinking."

Being pressed to answer usually made him squirm and change the subject. Speaking of his feelings and desires in their rich variety was never among his preferred activities. It took me a long time to understand that his preference for silence reflected a private rather than an evasive nature. I remember a conversation the morning after our first night together on the nubble, after I'd invited him to the island. Trying to get to know each other again after so many years, we were sitting on a log on the beach, running sand through our hands, awkwardly confessing our feelings about each other, when I asked him what were the most important or transforming events in his life. I was prepared to tell him the same about mine: moving to New York, having children, discovering feminism, becoming a writer. After a lot of prodding, he told me about mountain climbing, describing each of the highest peaks he had climbed on four continents. Not a word about his work, his marriage, or the sudden death of his son in a mental hospital, felled by an aneurysm at twenty-one. Only once in our two decades of living together did I ever see him cry over Freddy, the central focus of years of difficult existence and the likely cause of the demise of his first marriage. Returning home to our New York loft one winter evening after dusk, I found him standing near the window in the dark, one hand holding a highball, the other clenched in a fist raised toward the darkening sky, sobbing and calling out Freddy's name. Otherwise, he never mentioned him.

"That sounds right," says Scott when I read him this scene.

"But why? Why do you think you never talked about Freddy?"

"Compartmentalization, I guess," he says, falling silent again.

After four weeks in the ICU, Scott trades the breathing tube for a "trach collar," a device connected to the respirator, which is surgically inserted directly into his windpipe and contains a hole for a speaking valve. No more guessing at what he's trying to say. On his side, no more frustration at being misunderstood. Now we'll know.

The first words he utters, pointing to the sink: "Kleenex, please." Like a child's first word, a triumph. Thrilled and grinning, I hand him the small box of tissues from the edge of the sink. He wipes his nose.

Immediately my grin fades, as out of his mouth pours a great torrent of words, some comprehensible, some not, a wild river of stories, mixing events I know about with some I never heard of in our twenty years together. Can they be true? As a writer, I know I should be taking down every word of this momentous event, but I'm too excited, amazed, and alarmed to do anything but listen.

As news of this latest development spreads on the floor, one by one the doctors and nurses drift into Scott's room to witness the miracle and assess the damage. They question him closely to see what he knows of the past and of the present.

He knows his name and the date and city of his birth, but he doesn't know the current year, month, or season. He knows that my birthday is in August, but he can't remember my name. He knows we are in Maine but thinks the city we are in is San Francisco. He remembers that at age eighteen he left Cleveland for Duke to study biology, chemistry, and physics, but he claims to have gone to graduate school at Penn rather than Harvard. When asked if he knows what kind of building we are in, at first he guesses correctly, a hospital, and with his characteristic graciousness begins effusively thanking every nurse who enters the room. But moments later he decides we're in a university, UPenn in Philadelphia, where he says he used to work with Ralph Nader. (Can this possibly be true? He's never mentioned it before. Did Nader work in Philadelphia?) Whatever question is asked, he is never at a loss for an answer, however far-fetched. (This, from the man who taught me the virtue of silence, especially when dealing with people in authority.) To one doctor's question he replies that he was born in Ecuador, one of many delusional responses that the doctors have no way of knowing are false. He often mistakes one word for another with a similar sound or a rhyme: sometimes he thinks we're in Honolulu—is this because "hospital" and "Honolulu" begin with the same syllable, or because he was once hospitalized in Honolulu?

Who is this disconnected person, with his weird mixture of sense and incoherence, as irrational as he is imaginative? The dignified, courtly man I love has emerged from his enforced silence a loquacious stranger—sometimes a clown, full of wild flights of wordplay that keep Heather and Norm and me howling with laughter, sometimes a garrulous, nonsensical, even dirty old man hitting on the nurses. *Fluent aphasia* is the name the doctors give to this uncontrollable verbal pandemonium, a result of damage to the brain's speech centers, by which, in place of the elusive, sought-after words, the lips spew forth a circuitous approximation that usually sounds like babble but sometimes hints at wisdom. Are the myriad substitute words that emerge arbitrary or telling? Since aphasia, of both the fluent and non-fluent varieties, is caused by bodily injury or disease and often disappears with time, it would seem to be purely physical, not psychological. Yet overlaying my modest husband there appears to be another man with multiple alien personalities—now outgoing and entertaining, now authoritative and managerial—and all of them named Scott York. Can his injury have transformed his very self, stricken deep into his identity? Or revealed a buried self I never knew?

His ability to correctly interpret what he sees is also out of whack. "Oh-oh, you won't believe this, but here comes a train

track," he says to me as a nurse pushes a large X-ray machine
past his room.

"No, honey, that's not a train, that's an X-ray machine," I assure him, "though" (trying my best to enter into his frame of
mind) "I suppose it does look a little like a train."

"Okay, if you want to believe that, it's up to you. But you
wouldn't want to put your little pinkie out there in front of it!"
And he grabs for my arm to pull me out of harm's way.

In the following days he valiantly tries out one scenario after another in an attempt to make sense of his incomprehensible surroundings: sometimes the hospital is a library and the
nurses librarians; he sends me off to the "stacks" to get the
"tomes." Seeing Tiger Woods on the overhead TV, he decides
the hospital is a golf club. Then it's a large corporation, of
which he's an officer, addressing the ICU staff as if they were
employees whose "efficiency" he wants to improve, reporting
on a complicated discussion he's just had with one of the
trustees. Then it's the post office, with the male nurse, Dan, as
the postman, whom he questions about his pay and benefits,
asking me (his secretary?) to make sure that the people who sell
stamps have "a good benefits package." After uncomprehendingly seeing on TV some of the Olympic Games interspersed
with musical commercials, he instructs me, "The next time you
put on one of these musical comedy things, make sure you send
me a copy of the workmen's contract. I'd like you to consider
making a financial investment in the owner of the script."
When I fail to respond appropriately, he dismisses me impa-
tiently, saying, "All right, for the rest of the day the playwright
is in charge of this melodrama." And one afternoon, seeing a
male nurse walk by wearing a yellow hospital gown, he says,
"Look! Here come the gendarmes, wearing their uniforms
with the gold braid." Never before have I heard him speak with
such verbal flourishes. Do they disclose sides of him he never

chose to reveal to me, or do they signify something entirely new—perhaps mad?

I am thrilled; I am appalled; I am terrified. The patient is disoriented and bewildered; he has no memory at all of the accident.

All the nurses and residents assure me that Scott is merely suffering from "ICU psychosis," a temporary condition that often afflicts people who spend weeks in intensive care, where the erasure of day and night combined with constant sleep interruptions and the use of powerful mind-altering drugs wreak havoc on the mind, inducing a state of extreme confusion. Everyone promises it will disappear as soon as he leaves the hospital. I cling to this hope until a speech therapist, after extensively testing him, finally tells me that in her opinion Scott's inability to remember where he is even for a moment is because his short-term memory is completely shattered as a result of his multiple brain injuries.

I know something of short-term memory loss. Since Scott had surgery to repair an aortic aneurysm a dozen years before in Honolulu, his memory has been slowly and gradually worsening. In the beginning I thought it was a failure of attention, and I demanded better, inaugurating our first important quarrel. When his best efforts didn't help, our quarrel worsened, until I began to wonder if there might not be something physically wrong with him, and he finally agreed to have a memory test. The results were mixed: he could not recall three words he'd been asked to remember a few minutes earlier, but he could easily count backward from 100 by 17 in record time and name in reverse order not only the most recent U.S. presidents, as requested, but nearly all of them. The tentative conclusion was that he had probably, but not certainly, begun a long, slow slide into dementia (Alzheimer's). Soon afterward the media began to report that a surgical patient who spends hours on a heart-lung machine may suffer permanent memory loss—the more time on the machine, the greater the chance of interrupting the flow of oxygen to the brain, causing lasting damage. During his heart surgery, Scott had been on that machine for seven hours. Nevertheless, a decade later, the rhythm of his life had changed little: he continued going to his sculpture studio every day, planning and executing ambitious projects, spending summers in the city while I was on the island, flying up to visit me in Maine or his daughter in Boston on occasional weekends, undaunted by the complexities of post–9/11 jet travel. But tasks that required remembering a host of new details—using a computer, handling finances, responding quickly enough to complicated telephone menus—became increasingly difficult for him. We adjusted to those changes easily. He gave up the computer, and I gradually took over the bills and travel arrangements. Not until last year did I insist for safety's sake that he spend the entire summer with me in Maine.

I ask the speech therapist how long she thinks this extreme memory failure will last. She studies my face, trying to assess my resilience before delivering her devastating verdict: "It could take years before we know the true extent of the damage."

Had Scott not been the sort of man who makes things happen, we might have remained for each other simply romantic memories of idealized youth. Instead, two weeks before 1984 was set to launch, he made the call that changed our destinies.

It was midmorning, and outside our windows Washington Square Park was covered with snow. My daughter, Polly, twenty (older than I was when I had my first summer fling with Scott), was curled up in the red chair with a book, spending Christmas break at home, while her brother, Ted, twenty-two, was on tour with the college chorus. "Home" to them was our rambling prewar apartment, which their father and I, in the midst of divorcing, had divided in two to postpone the fight over who would have to move out. I occupied the living room, dining room, kitchen, "maid's" room (Polly's room), and tiny bath; he had the light-filled corner room, which used to be my writing room, and the two bedrooms and baths. I used the kitchen entrance, he the main entrance, and partway down the long entrance hall we'd put up a wall with a door to keep our two sides separate.

I was in the disorder of my makeshift dining-room office, futiley trying to work, when the phone rang. As soon as I picked it up, I recognized that voice from another world announcing itself as Scott York's.

He said he would be in New York on Friday and wondered if we might get together. The previous time I'd spoken to him was more than thirty years before, in 1953, when I was a twenty-year old Columbia graduate student in philosophy, newly married to a graduate student in literature, living in a dingy one-room apartment in upper Manhattan, and Scott was in the navy. When his aircraft carrier docked at the Brooklyn Navy Yard, the first thing he did, he said, was call me up—only to hear me reluctantly confess that I was married. "Oh, too bad," he said sadly before delivering the obligatory congratulations. My sentiment exactly.

(As I read Scott this passage off my computer, he asks ruefully, "Why couldn't you have waited for me? Think of all the fun we could have had in those years if we'd been married to each other instead." But of course, we both know we couldn't have. Our aspirations and desires were too far out of sync and our experience of life too limited. In 1953 Scott wasn't ready to marry anyone, whereas I, like most of my middle-class cohort, had been determined to find my mate fast and get the thing over with. Marriage to each other back then, we agree more than fifty years later, would probably have been disastrous. And again we repeat our litany of how lucky we are to have experienced our disappointments and mistakes with our previous spouses, saving our wiser, freer ways for each other, when we could finally get it right.)

This time when Scott asked how I was, I was glad to be able to tell him that I was in the process of being divorced (though from a different husband than I'd had the first time he'd called), and he reported that he'd been divorced for eight years. Despite myself, a kittenish tone I hadn't used since the women's movement had given me better tools crept unbidden into my voice as we conversed. Polly, hearing something new, put down her book and listened.

Would I be free for dinner this Friday?

Yes indeed I would!

Five minutes later my father phoned me from Cleveland. "I hope you won't be angry," he said sheepishly, "but I gave your telephone number to Scott York."

"I know, Daddy, he just called me. Of course I'm not angry. Why would I be?"

"Your mother tells me I'm not supposed to give out your number to anyone."

"Yes, but Mom should know that wouldn't apply to *him*."

Friday arrived. Around five-thirty, as I was rushing home with last-minute groceries, Ray the doorman informed me that a visitor was waiting in the lobby. I remember kicking myself for not coming home ten minutes earlier and being ready for him.

That first moment is indelibly stamped on my mind; I can play it back at will, in slow motion or fast. The perfectly tailored navy blue coat stretched across broad, squared shoulders; the tall, lean body gracefully turning toward me—first the head with pale, thinning hair, sans pompadour, slicked back from a widow's peak like Fred Astaire's; the nostrils of the sharp, high-bridged nose slightly flared, the blue eyes twinkling as the lips part and spread in a smile: same fine-featured face now overlaid with three decades of life, etched with character and sporting a trim yellow mustache, followed by the outstretched arms.

Everyone changes. From what I could see, Scott had only improved: a combination of the shy athletic youth I knew and this debonair, patrician-looking man of fifty-five. The old attraction sparked into flames as he took one decisive step toward me. "Well hello there! Let me look at you!" he said, and reached for my groceries.

Seated across from each other in the two red chairs beside the fireplace, drinking the Montepulciano he'd brought, we couldn't take our eyes off each other. Between us on the coffee table was a plate of hors d'oeuvres I'd prepared, but—perhaps out of the same strange courtesy that once made him uneasy making love to me—he wouldn't touch the food, no matter how I urged him. Quickly we tried to fill each other in on three decades of personal history—I my feminist activism, my books, my two marriages and two children; he his stint in the navy, then Harvard on the GI Bill (first the Graduate Design School, then the Business School), marriage, two children, a boy and a girl—

But, he said, lowering his eyes, his son had died some years ago.

Excruciatingly awkward silence. "Oh. I'm so sorry. How did he die?" I managed.

"He died in a mental hospital."

Silence still more excruciating.

Graciously he rescued me from my embarrassment by resuming his story: after graduate school a detour to produce movies for the literary critic I. A. Richards; painting in his spare time; and finally launching himself in the world of finance, from which he was now planning to take early retirement to become a full-time artist.

To do that, I thought, he had to be either very restless, very gutsy, or very successful.

As we talked, I was enchanted to trace the past in the present, that fascinating overlay, like looking up at the stars and knowing that their light shines down from the distant past. I feared that this exhilarating conjunction of then and now was as fragile as archaeological fragments that require technical expertise to handle. I wanted to disperse the accumulation of time's obscuring dust with a fine sable brush, dig into the past by the teaspoonful, slowly and carefully enough to preserve it.

He still preferred to listen rather than talk, forthcoming only when I pressed my questions. Yes, he answered, he was currently involved with a woman, someone with whom he liked to travel and whom he was meeting in Rome in three days' time. But no, he intended never to remarry.

I told him that I too had had it with marriage. I didn't mention my current romantic obsession, an opposite sort of man from Scott, far too wild, unreliable, and young for me, from whom I'd already begun the painful process of disentangling myself.

Polly, barefoot, though just outside the windows a snowstorm was strafing the streetlights with relentless rounds of snowflakes, pulled up a chair, crossed her legs in her lap, and listened.

❧

August is almost over, and Scott is still in the ICU, but I can see him growing stronger by the day. When he presses his hands against mine, he can almost push mine down. ("Not your standard seventy-five-year-old," according to one of his doctors.) With nurses holding him up on either side he's able to take several assisted steps. Once the feeding tube is removed, he manages to feed himself. I bring him pastries from our favorite bakery on Congress Street. Finally he's moved out of the ICU to a "step-down" unit on another floor, and I begin making plans to fly him back to New York for rehab. My heart is set on the Rusk Institute of New York University Hospital in Manhattan, which I've heard is the best rehab facility in the East. If he can recover anywhere, it must be there. No parent agonizing over college admissions can match my anxiety to get Scott into Rusk—hardly a sure thing, given their requirement that he be able to manage four hours a day of exercise and follow simple directions, neither of which seems even remotely possible. When a friend offers to put in a word for Scott with someone he knows at Rusk, I immediately abandon my high-minded strictures against pulling strings and gratefully accept.

At last I receive word that he will be admitted on August 30, five weeks and four days after the accident and the very day that the Republican National Convention convenes a few blocks west of Rusk to nominate George W. Bush for a second term. With the Iraq War becoming bloodier every day, all our friends are planning daily protest demonstrations, with banners and signs and strategies—demonstrations Scott and I had eagerly looked forward to joining, before the accident. For a moment I envy our friends their engagement with the world. But then I recall myself: my world is elsewhere now.

THREE

The Calling

Doctors told me that Scott would need a whole year to heal.

At first I was stunned. An entire year! Longer than it takes to make a child. But then I settled down. After all, a year is the length of an average teaching gig, only half as long as a stint in the Peace Corps, and far less time than it takes me to write a book. At our age a year can whiz by as fast as a screaming ambulance.

I signed on without a moment's hesitation. For one whole year my life would be aflame with purpose, single-minded and clear—to reclaim his life. There was no one else to do it and nothing else remotely worth doing. It became my mission, my passion, my obsession, displacing every other. All the skills and discipline I'd developed during decades of writing and activism retooled to serve my new calling. I sprang into action, powered by hope and adrenaline.

The problem was I got it wrong. What the various doctors actually said was that healing could continue for up to a year, for more than a year, for two or three years, possibly for the rest of his life, since every brain is different, and when the healing had run its course it would slow down and stop. No predictions about his condition afterward. Of their assorted messages, somehow only those about improvement registered, which I announced to our friends via e-mail as complete recovery within twelve months. But the shadow meaning of the doctors' words, that anything could happen, including the worst, and might take a very long time to discern—that in the end nothing was known—passed over my head, so strong is the human need for hope. "Dream's friend, illusion's sister," a Chinese poet calls it. Some people are temperamentally given to always expect the worst, but for me, with hope ever my drug of choice, I heard only what I needed or could bear to hear and took my solemn yearlong vow.

Then what am I to do with the news that awaits me and my son when we arrive at NYU Hospital, the medical parent of Rusk, on Scott's first morning there, that during the previous night—the very night he was admitted!—he had fallen off a gurney and injured his head *again*, winding up with new swellings and fresh bleeds in his brain?

He greets me wide-eyed with fright. "Did you hear what happened to me? I fell on my head again!"

I am beside myself with rage and helplessness. How could such a thing happen?

Explanations come only in passive voice. He "was left" on a gurney somewhere "upstairs" awaiting a test and "was found" on the floor, alone. The favored explanation is that he arrived on a weekend, when staff is low—everyone knows that things can go wrong there on weekends—shifting responsibility to me for bad timing. All rehab therapies are suspended while they try to determine the new damage. His nurse advises me to watch him closely every moment and to hire a private-duty nurse to sit beside him through the night, since he's not safe alone even for a second.

We had built our bond on our independence and autonomy; they were (paradoxically) part of what drew us together, what we had in common. His other women all wanted more of him than he could offer, more and more. I alone wanted less. And now I must never let him out of my sight.

All around us, up and down the corridor, I see patients left to cope alone without advocates or hope. Suddenly I'm acutely aware of them: an elderly stroke patient who fills the halls with his loud, plaintive howls; a young woman with broken hips who begs me, as I pass her room, to send someone—anyone—to help her out of bed; Scott's roommate with Parkinson's, a once-successful music producer, according to the decades-old profile of him from *Ebony* magazine that he posts on the door, who will be discharged to a nursing home because he has no one to care for him. Between their fates and Scott, I plant myself like an impenetrable, thorny hedge.

The worse things go for him, the greater my resolve to make them better. I read each frustration as an invitation to act. When I discover that the night nurse has automatically put Scott into diapers, though he's shown no sign of incontinence, I make sure it never happens again. When new tests are scheduled, I insist on accompanying him. When he lacks the energy to eat, I feed him. My hope, my tenacity, my fierce optimistic bias summon the hidden reserves of energy, physical and mental, I will need to bring him back. With intense allegiance, I count every sign of his improvement a victory and every disappointment or frustration a mere temporary impediment on the road to recovery. Unlike the speech therapist, who sees a problem in his response to her instructions to write down his name and address, I'm triumphant as he writes:

Scott York Scott Roland York in love
I must focus my mind on new thoughts

The therapist redirects his attention by writing ADDRESS on his paper. And again I rejoice as he writes our address perfectly, complete with zip code. Similarly, when he answers a doctor's question about what year we're in by saying, "The year George W. Bush will be taken down," I overlook his temporal failing in order to celebrate his successful finesse.

Not that I'm ignorant about his condition. Having always appeased my demons with lavish feasts of information, each night before sleep I fight despair by searching the Internet to see what's in store for us. I'm back in school again, focused, charged, sleep-deprived, as I push myself to absorb the obscure intelligence on which our future depends. On a dozen websites all the symptoms and consequences of brain trauma are laid out systematically, scientifically: the disabling loss of memory, the general confusion, the attention deficit, the incapacity to follow instructions, the complete inability to plan or organize or even just know to put your pants on before your shoes ("sequencing problems"); the impulsive outbursts ("disinhibition") that lead some sufferers to rage and curse at their caregivers or talk dirty to strangers; the bouts of agitation; the total blackout about the accident itself; and the evening delirium ("sundowning") that produces delusions, fixations, hallucinations, and paranoia in the cognitively impaired, particularly the elderly, in unfamiliar surroundings. This strange temporary madness has been shown to be related to disturbances of the body's circadian rhythms (observed in body temperature, heart rate, hormone secretion, and other physiological responses), and perhaps also to the brain's sensitivity to light, which may account for such disparate effects as jet lag and winter depression and may be exacerbated by anesthesia and the medications administered for pain and anxiety.

But along with the tough news, the dread diagnoses and prognoses are invariably enveloped in a rosy aura of hope, which I inhale like cocaine: given enough therapy, stimulation, and time, the symptoms will diminish—once he's home the sundowning will fade; his stamina will increase and his fatigue lessen; the fog filling his head will gradually lift; with repetition he'll relearn how to walk and to dress; and even lacking memory and awareness, he'll be able to take pleasure in the experience of each moment before promptly forgetting it.

☙

One night, reading about traumatic brain injury (TBI) as I troll the Internet, I come upon something ominously called "Second Impact Syndrome":

> Also termed "recurrent traumatic brain injury," [it] can occur when a person sustains a second brain injury before the symptoms of the first traumatic brain injury have healed . . . The second impact is more likely to cause brain swelling and widespread damage . . . Death can occur rapidly . . . The long-term effects of recurrent brain injury can be muscle spasms, rapidly changing emotions, hallucinations, and difficulty thinking and learning.

This syndrome is usually invoked to describe motorcyclists, boxers, and football players, who choose to risk such injuries, not patients in a leading hospital. Again, I am plunged into gloom. It hardly comforts me (or helps Scott) that a week later the hospital concludes its "internal investigation" of his newest fall by admitting that it "erred," conceding that it never should have left him unguarded, should have given him upon admission a red bracelet to indicate that the patient has "safety issues," should have protected him. They didn't, so I must. Yet not even a red bracelet, which I finally manage to get him, or round-the-clock one-on-one care can guarantee his safety. As every reader of fairy tales knows, your fate lies waiting for you where you least expect it, and there is nothing you can do to evade it.

Not one week later, returning from the cafeteria where I'd slipped off for a cup of coffee while he slept, I find his bed empty. My stomach lurches; I rush to the nurses' station.

"Where's my husband?" I demand.

He's been taken to the Swallowing Lab on the third floor for another test—"but don't worry," says his nurse, "I sent along an aide with orders not to leave him alone."

In a flash I'm on those stairs, taking them two at a time up to the third floor. I dash through a long hallway and into the Swallowing Lab just as the lab assistant is leaving the room. Oblivious of the red bracelet, apparently unaware that Scott is confused and unable to follow instructions, she's left him un-attended on a very high chair in front of the X-ray machine, straps hanging loose beside him and no one else around. A moment more and he'd have fallen on his head *again*, this time from an even greater height. *Twenty minutes* pass before anyone returns to the room.

Why is there no safety warning on the front of his chart?

Where is the aide who was instructed not to leave him?

How will he survive in this place?

When I find the aide in the third-floor visitors' room watching TV, she explains that she was ordered to wait for Scott here, and how could she, a mere aide, on the lowest rung of the hierarchy, protest?

Now I'm a lioness stalking prey. Notebook in hand, I ques-tion everyone I see—lab assistant, receptionist, nurses, doctor—writing conspicuously, as if preparing a case, and bristle when stonewalled. Except for the lowly aide, who lacks authority, not one person on the floor was aware that Scott needed guarding. And not one person besides me seems distressed about it. Each one blames someone else.

After that I don't dare let down my guard for a moment, even though, with the specter of *lawsuit* newly hanging in the air, Scott and I are suddenly VIPs, with metal cutlery in place of plastic, food enough for two, frequent reassuring visits from the head nurse. I become a dervish of intervention, exhilarated, wired, back on the barricades, meeting, analyzing, advocating, protesting. In my commitment to save him, I'm like one possessed. For twelve hours a day I watch over him, sharing his meals, wheeling him to his appointments, sitting in on his therapies, barely ever letting him out of my sight until he's in bed for the night. On weekends, when all therapy stops, I wheel him down to the Glass Garden, a humid tropical greenhouse with flowering bromeliads, palm trees, giant goldfish, and noisy tropical birds, which is tucked behind a side entrance to the hospital. Scott, whose injured brain is quickly overloaded with new sensations, is ready to leave two minutes after we arrive, but for me the piercing birdsong and lush scents that fill the air of this unlikely refuge lift my spirits, which rise higher still with each of his small triumphs—his unexpected recognition of a friend, his pleasure watching the East River boat traffic from the cafeteria window—and never mind the crazy nonsense talk that frightens visitors, the irrational refusals, the terrifying sundowning that overcomes him when dusk descends, as if he'd been bitten by a vampire, leaving him plagued by hallucinations and madness.

I cling to my optimism, my hope. But each night back home in our loft the terrors await me. What dread event will happen to him next? What will become of him? Of us? Of me? Sometimes I cry myself to sleep, allowing my hope to die down to embers until, come dawn, I manage to stoke it up again for the coming day. An e-mail from my trusted doctor-cousin cautions me: "Although you can't reverse serious brain damage, your own spirit, optimism, and strength will be among the most important factors influencing Scott's outcome. Only your loving support can allow healing to achieve its maximal benefit." Despite insufficient sleep or food (no time, no appetite), on the long walk back to the hospital I feel myself gradually revive for the day's inevitable battles, invigorated by the sheer energy of the traffic and the ubiquitous smell of strong morning coffee. The cacophony of commerce raising its grates and unlocking its doors reminds me that the world I once inhabited is, as always, out there turning straw into gold   without us.

One day I lower the guardrail on Scott's bed and stretch out beside him to listen to jazz CDs through earphones, one on his ear, one on mine.

Seeing us lying in bed together, the nurses grow shy and pull the curtain around us. Do they think we need privacy from the other patients in the room in order to listen to Miles Davis? Phillip, our social worker, stares at us in wonder: "In all my years working in hospitals," he says, "you are the first couple I've ever seen in bed together." The young nurses' aides grow suddenly curious about us and ask how long we've been together. I give them the long answer: fifty-four years since we fell in love, thirty-four years of separation, twenty years since we got back together. They go mushy over the amorous septuagenarian couple—until they get used to us in bed and stop pulling the curtain.

But after dark, when I must leave, a different image of us emerges. Scott is certain that the minute I go, I'll be killed in traffic or mugged on the street, never to return. He tries to keep me from leaving, pleads, cajoles, panics—till the doctors prescribe antianxiety meds and, when those don't work, antipsychotic meds as well. But nothing calms him. He can't remember where he is, where I am, or, given his complete loss of all sense of time, what "back tomorrow" can mean. Sometimes

I arrive home to find desperate messages from him on my answering machine (he's inveigled the night nurse into dialing), and sometimes in the middle of the night or early hours of the morning he calls again in a panic, begging me to return. With breaking heart I try to talk him down and reassure him, barely able to wait until morning to rush back to his sterile, fluorescent-lit room in time for his breakfast. Then what joy to see his face light up as he cries, "You're here!" and mercifully forgets that I was ever away.

As he is oblivious of what will happen when the sun goes down again, I refuse to imagine what awaits us when the fabled year of healing is up.

Scott's medical "team" is immense. In addition to his rehab therapists (physical, speech, occupational, and cognitive), plus a staff of nurses and social workers, he is attended by specialists in trauma, physiatry, psychiatry, neurology, neurosurgery, orthopedics, cardiology, pulmonary disease, and swallowing disorders, some of whom are frequently at war with one another. The cardiologist and the neurosurgeon duke it out over the dosage of Scott's blood thinner, Coumadin, which is supposed to dissolve the blood clots that tend to form on artificial heart valves like his but which also increases the danger of excess bleeding. The neurologist opposes the memory drugs prescribed by the psychiatrist, who opposes the antianxiety drugs prescribed by the physiatrist. Most members of the team seem competent enough, and some are superb, but given Scott's complex and still unstable condition, I know that a single bad one could mean sudden death.

I decide to get a second opinion about the overall treatment plan. I ask around until I identify the "best" neurologist in town and invite him for a consultation. On the following Saturday he visits Scott's bedside, examines his chart, runs through the familiar neurological routine of manual maneuvers ("touch your nose with your left index finger . . ."), and asks the standard test questions for memory and cognitive capacity, plus some new ones ("Can you spell the following words backward?"). After fifteen minutes he tells me that he will recommend withholding all the psychotropic medications Scott has been getting for agitation and for sleep ("Let's not muddle up his brain any more than necessary," he says in explanation), but otherwise continuing his current treatment. As someone who's barely willing to take an aspirin, I cheer this change. But the neurologist's orders in the chart are so illegible that I must do battle with the evening nurse to make sure she discontinues the offending pills.

One morning, while I'm voicing a complaint about one doctor to another doctor, I discover that I have the authority to discharge from the case anyone I choose. Armed by this belated revelation of my powers, I immediately begin to fire incompetents.

First the psychiatrist, who has declared Scott "depressed" after one minute's observation of him lying listlessly in bed and one question about his appetite.

Incredulous, I follow him down the hall to inquire how he can diagnose depression on the basis of a single question.

"It's not based on that question alone."

"Then what else?"

"I can tell he's depressed by his facial expression."

For a patient with a breathing tube in his windpipe, who cannot walk, who is down fifty pounds, and who doesn't know the month, the year, where he is, or the name of his own daughter—a lack of appetite and his facial expression reveal his problem to be *depression*?

Fired.

A week later I take on the clueless psychologist, whose fast, mumbled speech and refusal to make eye contact with Scott make it impossible for him to understand her test instructions, leaving him frustrated and angry.

Fired.

After the mishap in the Swallowing Lab, I seek out the nurse who sent him upstairs without adequate precautions, the same nurse who was in charge of his case on the night of his admission, when he fell from the gurney.

Fired.

Thus am I able to maintain my belief in his recovery within the year.

I wasn't always so unambivalently optimistic about him. His reappearance in my life in 1984 had filled me with conflict. In our youth we'd set off in opposite directions and traveled so long and far on our chosen paths that by the simple rules of geometry we must be worlds apart. Yet as I spotted him waiting for me at the Denver airport in September of 1984, the old attraction was stronger than ever.

Several weeks earlier I'd accepted a last-minute offer to be visiting writer in residence at the University of Colorado at Boulder, my first full-salaried university job, complete with benefits and the use of a small nineteenth-century cottage up in the mountains. The next time Scott called to ask me out to dinner in New York and I had to decline because I was moving, he gallantly offered instead to meet my plane in Denver and spend the weekend helping me get settled. Since he lived roughly midway between New York and Boulder, I figured it made little difference to him whether he courted me toward the East or toward the West. Not so, however, to me, for whom his offer produced a minor crisis: how tempting it would be to sink into the luxury of his attentions and permit him to save me. But having just escaped from a husband and a lover, wouldn't it be cowardly to plunge into a new relationship before seeing what Colorado had to offer? Though sweet and rather touching, Scott was provincial and probably dull—perhaps as inappropriate for me, in an opposite way, as the lover I'd just fled. As we left Denver for Boulder in a rental car, I was relieved that unlike my husband, who was a demon driver, Scott was considerate, careful, dependable. But were those traits suitable for the nervy activist-adventurer I fashioned myself? Despite my ambivalence, we got so engrossed in our conversation that we missed our turnoff—as we invariably would every time we were on the road together. Okay, scratch *dull*.

Everything there was new to me. At fifty-two, I'd never before rented a house by myself (my time alone at the summerhouse in Maine didn't count, since in prior years I'd often gone there with my family); I'd never climbed a mountain or seen a desert; and now, seated on the terrace of a sunlit café, breathing thin mountain air and consuming meltingly flaky croissants with perfectly layered lattes, I was being instructed in mountain living by a seasoned member of the Explorers Club. He was arranging the salt and pepper shakers, sugar bowl, napkins, and cutlery into a diagram of a mountain meadow in order to reassure me and build up my confidence—an approach that was also new to me. During decades of New York feminist politics and a confrontational marriage, my style had become adversarial, whereas Scott was consummately agreeable. How to respond? Without an adversary, where would I find the edge? Since I could no longer play the discredited girly game, how could I win?

Until dinnertime he helped me with my chores: hanging curtains on my sunporch, fixing up my kitchen, and at my suggestion buying music for lovemaking. As we walked into the music store, a lush recording of Bach's Air on the G String filled the room. It was from a tape made up entirely of adagios from every musical period. Although I would never before have considered buying such a compilation, cutting off one movement from the rest of a work, I abandoned my purity in the service of sex. Not one day out of Manhattan and I was already . . . *compromising my principles* or *lightening up*? How could I tell?

On Sunday, the day Scott was to leave, the English department was giving a party for new faculty. Family and friends were invited, but I was so eager to appear autonomous that I asked Scott if he'd mind dropping me off around the corner and meeting me later, as if we were having an illicit affair. That agreeable man chose to indulge my ambivalence by dismissing my behavior as mere eccentricity and obliged me.

As single-mindedly devoted as I am now to healing Scott, so he was then to winning me. He pursued me with traditional romantic gestures that at first I found laughable, then endearing, and finally irresistible: the nightly phone calls, the roses delivered weekly to my cottage, the weekend trips to Santa Fe, New Orleans, San Francisco, and, over Christmas break, all the way to Jerusalem—a place I'd never considered visiting until he produced the tickets as an act of solidarity with my ethnic roots.

The expense of those trips, which I could not have afforded on my own, became a subject of daring negotiation. He would have preferred to foot every bill, but for me, committed to equality, such an arrangement would have been hypocritical. Instead, we worked out a plan whereby I contributed a third and he two-thirds of our common expenses, roughly the same proportion as our incomes—and, as it turned out, also of our assets. This awkward experiment moved us subtly closer to . . .

What? Not marriage, surely, which we had both renounced.

Besides, I wasn't yet divorced. Then what? Living together? Way premature. Perhaps some provisional or conditional commitment . . . ?

Over drinks in our hotel in the Israeli resort town of Elat, Scott cleared his throat and took my hand to declare, "If you ever decide that you'd like to get married, I want you to know I'd be willing." His seriousness about me was flattering, it took my breath away, but still I demurred.

He said no more. Unthreatened by my feminism, in fact turned on by it, he asked for a copy of my syllabus for my Introduction to Women's Literature course, and week by week he eagerly read my class assignments: Virginia Woolf, Zora Neale Hurston, Maxine Hong Kingston, Marilynne Robinson, Alice Walker, Alice Munro. He was my most ardent student. Night after night on the telephone our connection tightened as we pursued the meanings of love, sex, money, equality, and now literature too.

So here's to long-distance courtship!—the best way to get to know a person without plunging in over your head. A way to ensure that even though he takes your breath away, you'll be able to breathe. A way to work out in advance potential glitches so that when you finally fill your lungs to capacity and take the plunge, you can resurface in record time and begin to swim.

Maybe every romance is essentially the same, with its stages, analogous to those of death and mourning. The beginnings, all self-presentation. The breathless courtship, with its fantasy and promise. The period of rational assessment: Who is this person? How can this last? The period of apprehensive ambivalence and testing, when elation and anxiety alternately rise up like the powerful arms of a windmill to agitate the air. The hesitant try-out. Then the ultimate test, the attempted breakup, with tears and regrets, which, if survived, leads directly to . . . : the consummation, with commitment to lasting love.

Given our long separations, it took us a while to complete all the stages—exactly long enough that by the time my Boulder stint was up, Scott was ready to follow me to New York.

If he was willing to relocate his entire life to be with me, the least I could do was keep my recurring ambivalence to myself. While I stalled for time by spending the summer alone in Maine, my resolute lover arranged to be transferred to his firm's New York office, high up in the World Trade Center; and by the time the weather turned, he was already scouting out downtown lofts for a place where, within walking distance of his office, we could merge the motley contents of two disparate lives and try to fit them together.

One Wednesday evening in the last week of September, eleven weeks after the accident, as we are finishing our dinner in Scott's room, Phillip the social worker joins us to announce that ten minutes earlier at a staff meeting Scott's discharge date was set for Friday, with a strong recommendation of twenty-four-hour home care.

Friday! That's the day after tomorrow! Nothing is ready!

I turn on Phillip. "How can you do this? You told me I'd have two weeks' notice, not two days!" Tears are welling in my eyes.

Phillip seems genuinely taken aback. "Not to worry," he says gently.

Not worry? But we're completely unprepared. No grab bars in the shower, no idea what other equipment we'll need, no place set up for the aide, and I haven't even begun to look for the right person.

"That's no problem," Phillip assures me. "I can get you a list of agencies that'll send someone the next day."

"Without an interview? I can't hire someone to live with us I haven't interviewed."

He scratches his head. Evidently he's never heard of an advance interview. "If you don't like who they send, they'll send someone else. Or you call a different agency."

Scott is getting agitated, seeing my distress. So I invite Phillip to step into the hall, where I tell him exactly what I think of him and his policy of kicking out an improving patient without adequate notice. "How can you treat people so heartlessly?"

"But I assure you, we aren't treating your husband any differently than we treat anyone else. This is standard operating procedure."

Every word he says only increases my outrage. "Precisely!" I fling back at him.

But Phillip is not the culprit. Though no one will admit it, the wheels of discharge have been activated by the strict rules of Medicare reimbursements and once set in motion can't be stopped, only sometimes slowed down a bit. I am grateful when the hospital's patient representative slips me a telephone number and the specific magic words to use to win us a few days' reprieve.

Again I rush into action, telephoning, interviewing, ordering, arranging—though those few extra days are not nearly enough to prepare for a smooth transition home.

Scott picks up my anxiety. "They're keeping me a prisoner here," he confides to me the next morning upon my arrival. Then he lowers his voice to ask, "Do you know where they're keeping the hostages?"

I try to reassure him. "There are no hostages. You're not a prisoner. We're going home soon. This is not a prison."

"In that case I am going to the lobby to see the manager of this hotel. I insist on seeing the manager!" And for the first

time, in violation of the liability-driven hospital rules, he aban-
dons the wheelchair to which he's been confined, except when
accompanied by a physical therapist, and walks out of his room
unassisted.

I follow him down the hall. "Wait! Where are you going?"

Sternly, throwing off my hands: "I'm going to place a phone
call to Manila."

"But sweetheart, we're in New York, and this is a hospital."

He shakes his head and says, "I am the ultimate arbiter of all
misconceptions."

It's in his final session with the speech therapist that he gives
his first sign of awareness that something may not be completely right with him. In the poetic vocabulary of his fluent
aphasia, so distant from his lifelong verbal concision, he asks the
therapist, "Do you have any words of wisdom that will evapo-
rate all these ills?" And "Are we ever going to get through this
travail?"

His awareness that something is wrong, called "insight" in
the brain injury lexicon, is considered a sign of healing, which
leads to the irony that the more insight he has, the sadder he
feels—and the less insight he has, the sadder I feel.

In our few remaining days at Rusk, Scott's physical and occupational therapists offer me crash training in how to help
him negotiate stairs, maneuver in and out of taxis, step safely
into and out of the shower, manage a cane, a walker, a wheelchair—until, by the end of the week, though I'm full of trepi-
dation and fear, I feel at the same time an almost exhilarating
eagerness to move this odyssey to the next level and see what
happens once we return . . .

FOUR

Home

Home! No more separate beds or nights apart, no more anguished middle-of-the-night phone calls. Now I have sole control. That might be a scary prospect for some people, but I have always relished control as my way of coping with contingency. Although the price is high—being on twenty-four-hour watch and exclusively responsible for what may go wrong—it's worth it to be able to take full charge of his recovery.

I unlock the door while Barbara—a highly recommended home health aide who cared for a friend's parents until they died—pushes Scott's wheelchair into our loft, the same loft we've lived in for two decades. I watch his face for recognition. Does he notice the hospital bed in front of the window where my NordicTrack used to be, or the clunky commode newly installed beside our bed, or that the small rugs and tables have all been removed as trip hazards, replaced by his favorite leather armchair that I've brought home from his studio? As he looks around, bewildered, I doubt it. Meticulous attention to detail—a quality that got him through graduate school, served as the foundation of a successful financial career, and transformed him into an artist—is now so far beyond him that on a standard attention-building exercise designed for the brain injured, requiring that he cross out all the *if*s and *and*s in a simple text, he misses more than half of them.

High-ceilinged and vast, with a wall of eight tall windows and old oak flooring that's just right for dancing on, our loft, converted from a turn-of-the-century printing factory, is as open and free as we ourselves aspired to be back in 1986 when we first moved in. As soon as I quashed my ambivalence about our living together, Scott engaged several New York real estate agents to line up properties and flew into town for two packed weekends of loft hunting. With his usual executive dispatch he planned to pare down the options before I returned from Maine.

Combining his high aesthetic standards with my requirements that I have an inviolable private space to work in and that I be able to pay my share, Scott had narrowed the choices to three by the time I returned to the city in September. We had pretty much decided on a large fixer-upper near Chinatown—whose main virtue was that attached to it was a small, separate apartment with its own entrance, which could serve as my work space—when Scott agreed to let the agent show us one more loft she'd been unable to schedule earlier.

As soon as we walked in, we knew this was the one. Bathed in afternoon sunlight, pristine and elegant, with high, arched ceilings, graceful columns, and one charming curved wall, it was essentially a single huge room. The only completely closed-off space was the bathroom. Owned and designed by a talented young architect who worked for I. M. Pei, it needed nothing except a paint job and some bookcases before we could move in. "Take it!" whispered our friend Susan the moment she stepped inside.

I was torn between beauty and practicality, pleasure and privacy. "Don't worry, we'll construct a private room for you," promised Scott, who had studied architecture at Harvard. But like a tightly written poem, the space was too perfect to risk marring with wanton change.

My previous marriage had foundered on secrecy and concealment. At the end we had built a wall dividing our lives in two. Now I clung to my dream of establishing my life with Scott on a basis of openness and trust. Perhaps we should forget about constructing walls? Could one live by a dream? Rashly, in a flight of audacity and faith, I decided to risk it.

We moved into the loft in October, furnishing it half with his things, half with mine. Not that we took our wall-less state as a mandate to merge our lives. On the contrary, we continued to immerse ourselves in projects so private that the other hardly knew what they were until completed—whereupon we each became the other's staunchest fan. Thus it is that in every empty spot along the walls of our loft and on all the windowsills sit Scott's sculptures of marble, alabaster, wood, or bronze, admiringly arranged by me; and in a glass-enclosed bookcase between two windows is a shelf of leather-bound, gold-edged presentation copies of my published books, one copy of each, mostly commissioned by him. We shared our dinners, walks, weekends, travels, and our bed, but our days and thoughts remained our own. My faith was not misplaced: the entire loft quickly became my writing space, at least from 8:00 a.m., when Scott conscientiously left the apartment, until 5:00 p.m., when he returned—even after he traded his World Trade Center office for a small sculpture studio. Since then, except when we've gone away, hardly a day and certainly no week has passed that we haven't sat on a sofa in the early evening to bask in the openness of our giant room, watching the setting sun cast moving shadows of our plants and Japanese paper lanterns onto the lone curved wall—until now.

The buzzer rings. Bearing grapes and quantities of sushi, our dear friends Ann, Danny, and Linda come to celebrate the homecoming. Scott, social skills intact though his cognitive skills have failed, automatically assumes his role of gracious host. From his seat he offers drinks and makes entertaining patter as if he'd never been away. In fact, he has no memory of having been away. At the first mention of *hospital*, where he's just spent three intense months, he says, perplexed, "What hospital?"

I choose to interpret this lapse to mean that the hospital is now behind us. I am convinced of it when, as night begins to fall, instead of going crazy he simply goes to sleep.

The regimen of care mapped out by the doctors follows the Medicare reimbursement limits: sixty days of home therapies— physical, speech, and occupational—after which he must be re-assessed, followed by outpatient therapies for as long as he continues to improve. The doctors have also prescribed, and Medicare will support, round-the-clock home health aides for up to sixty days.

The aides soon become my nemesis. Not only because I am reluctant to risk Scott's recovery by delegating his care to complete unknowns, but, having always been deeply uncomfortable with the idea of household help of any kind, how can we suddenly invite outsiders into our lives to serve us—and at a time when we are so vulnerable? Frazzled by twenty-four-hour "assistance," I don't know what to do with these strangers in our midst, from supercompetent Barbara, who comes in every weekday between 2:00 and 7:00 p.m., to the ever-changing aides an agency sends to cover the morning shift, the weekends, and, worst of all, the nights, when someone sits in the dark beside our bed watching us sleep. I am distraught by their invasive and relentless presence, oppressed by their ever-observing eyes. Once the therapies, each thrice a week, begin, plus the nurses, the aides, and the phlebotomist who draws Scott's blood early every morning to test his clotting time, which determines the correct dose of his blood thinner, our loft feels like Grand Central Station. Sleep deprived and tense, I jump like a nerve in a decaying tooth whenever the door buzzer screeches.

Still, I cannot do everything myself; unquestionably, I need help, if for nothing more than to watch over Scott while I'm in the bathroom or on the telephone or out shopping for groceries. Only while he naps can I sometimes slip off to my desk to attack my mounting pile of bills, reports, and insurance forms, pretending to be invisible for a few minutes at a time. If I stay at my desk much longer, he'll sleep too long, leaving me feeling remiss for failing to keep him, as prescribed, "alert and stimulated."

Longingly I wait for the moment when the hovering helpers will depart and, for a brief while between shifts, leave us alone together—as longingly as I once awaited the moment when he himself would leave at eight o'clock each morning to fulfill his mantras: *out the door!* and *get the job done.* As with everything he did, it was partly for me and partly for himself that he left me alone. The very week he pulled off his long-planned early retirement from the world of finance at the age of fifty-eight, he began to design, blueprint, and then, with the help of an island carpenter, build a studio for me at the nubble in Maine, to ensure my privacy even when he was there. That accomplished, he turned directly to his own long-postponed ambitions: he found a shared sculpture studio not far from our loft, where he spent eight, sometimes ten hours a day, transforming large blocks of marble into sculptures that from the very start bore his distinctive style. Wary of impinging on each other's space, we worked out ways to be both together and apart, perfect counterparts in self-sufficiency.

And now our solitude and freedom have been reduced to mere abstractions, as all privacy is wiped out and his disability renders him utterly dependent, making prisoners of us both.

Could I, as certain well-intentioned friends suggested, have cut loose by turning him over to someone else's care? ("You mustn't let him take you down with him"; "One accident shouldn't ruin two lives," they said, trying to protect me.) No, I could not. During his first crucial year post-accident, my single task, unquestioned and unexamined, is to maximize his healing by supervising his recovery down to the minutest detail. I have no time, no interest, no energy for anything else. If I have a moment to read, I read about TBI, traumatic brain injury. I read memoirs by people who recovered sufficiently to write a book about it. If I glance at a newspaper, my eye unfailingly ferrets out the report about survivors of strokes, blows, brain tumors, or accidents who suddenly awaken after years in a coma or recover their lost powers of speech to live fulfilling lives, and I close my eyes to the occasional stories about those, often celebrities, who never wake up again.

Anyway, whether I like it or not, he won't permit anyone but me in the bathroom with him; no one knows better than I what he likes to eat; I alone can detect subtle changes in his condition and anticipate his needs. He is mine, and I am his: all others are intruders whom I would never entrust him to and cannot wait to be rid of.

Recovery requires that Scott keep expanding his limits. Under the guidance of his inventive physical therapist, Ilsa Sandel, who comes to our apartment three times a week, he begins to move more confidently. Despite his walking problem with his left foot, whereby his toes hit the ground before his heel, making him shuffle dangerously, she quickly banishes the wheelchair, the walker, the cane. Next, drawing on his love of basketball, she constructs a hoop from a wire coat hanger, hangs it from the middle of our ceiling, and presents him with a large, soft ball to toss through the hoop to stretch his spine and improve his balance. Thus our loft, which over the years has accommodated meetings, dances, salons, book parties, and fund-raisers, adds ball court to its résumé. By her second week Ilsa is ready to take us outdoors. I am surprised, having unthinkingly assumed that he was far too fragile to leave our loft. On each visit she gets us to venture a little farther, pointing out all the stoops, benches, and flat-topped Siamese sprinklers where Scott can sit down to rest, until finally one day, with plenty of rest stops en route, we walk all the way to his studio in Union Square, eight blocks away.

In the studio, everything is as it was. Decades' worth of work covers every surface, every wall. Hearing him cogently answer Ilsa's questions as if he were still a working artist who had never suffered a near-fatal fall, I am confident that he may one day recover enough to return to his studio and resume art making—if not by himself then with a hired companion. The ultimate question asked by every doctor and therapist, the central question of rehab whose answer determines the course of treatment, is: What goals do you have for his recovery? To this I invariably reply: for him to be an artist again. As he rearranged his life to be able to live by art, so I believe art will be the key to his rehabilitation, however long it takes.

One Tuesday in mid-October, at Ilsa's urging, I arrange for our good friend Susan to meet us for lunch at a restaurant a block and a half away. This is a far cry from the weekly outings to distant corners of the city we launched soon after he became an artist, when, instead of knocking off work on weekends, we had a regular Tuesday "date" to take the subway to some unfamiliar neighborhood and explore the streets like tourists, sampling the local wares and ethnic food, returning home to a nightcap of dancing and lovemaking. But in some ways today's outing is far more adventurous. For the brain injured, an hour of sitting through a meal in a New York restaurant with a hurting back and a brain bombarded with stimuli can quickly result in a catastrophic overload that brings on exhaustion or collapse. The sounds, the movement, the lights, the conversation, the people, the menu, the waiters, the food can be way too much to process at one sitting. But to expand his limits, I'll risk it.

Shortly after noon we set off. Bundled up, his left foot shuffling, this athlete, who in his sixties twice took off in hot pursuit of teenage pickpockets, chasing them down many blocks to the finish rather than be victimized, just manages with my help to cross an avenue and two side streets, negotiate the crowded sidewalk, and descend the four steps into the restaurant without mishap.

Inside, Susan greets us excitedly. We pile all our coats on the back of Scott's chair for extra padding. When the menu proves too baffling, I order for him. Susan and I converse as if this were a normal lunch, but I am excruciatingly aware of the difference. Since the point of everything I do is its effect on Scott, other activities—like lunching with a friend or exchanging gossip—feel like a mere semblance of ordinary life, which has begun to seem unreal to me. Nothing I do or say can make the real coincide with the sham or hide the difference between who I am now and who I was before. It's as if there were an invisible screen between me and the world.

Once our order is placed, Scott's impatience, with TBI predictability, begins to mount. "Where's our waiter! What's keeping him?" But he eats lustily, managing two courses before the stimulation finally overwhelms him. We skip dessert and I call for the check. By the time we get home he's already forgotten the entire outing, but it's still a milestone on the road to normalcy, and I'm as thrilled as a mother at her child's first birthday. The subject line of my crowing e-mail to our friends says, "Scott out to lunch," and I begin the message: ". . . in the good sense."

After the nighttime aide dozes off for two nights running (which I'm able to observe because under her scrutiny I can't fall asleep), I have my excuse to let her go. Next, I reclaim our weekends. Later, growing bold, I dispense with the ever-changing morning aide, and finally, when Scott is able to walk without needing someone constantly at his elbow, I dismiss even our mainstay, Big Barbara, as Scott calls her, who after several months has become our friend and whose name he sometimes remembers. Before long, the home therapies too have run their course, and we find ourselves with a few precious weeks of privacy before the prescribed outpatient therapies begin. With the door buzzer and telephone silent at last, we celebrate our newfound freedom by sleeping late.

Eagerly I resume the household cooking, which has long been my special form of meditation—not only our dinners, as before, but now also breakfasts and lunches, which we take at the long oak table, with Scott as always the most appreciative of eaters. Only when I take over his job of washing up, which he had always faithfully executed in the name of domestic equality, does he seem disgruntled. But I have no choice: washing dishes is now far too complex a task for him to manage.

Sometimes we put on music and slow dance in the afternoons. In the evenings, piling pillows behind us in bed, we watch old movies on TV. So what if he can't fathom the plot, as long as he can lie contentedly beside me on the bed, holding my hand, while the familiar faces flicker across the screen, as if we were kids making out in the back row of the Cedar & Lee in Cleveland Heights. While we're cuddled up with bowls of frozen yogurt, I discover that there's more to enjoying movies than comprehension. If it doesn't bother him that he doesn't know what's going on and forgets the movie the minute it's over, it doesn't bother me that my wry commentaries go over his head. In truth, he was never much of a critic. When he kisses my hand and says for the hundredth time, "I can't believe how lucky we are," I know it's not the brain injury talking, because in that moment I feel the same.

The ideal of care I aspire to is the anti–nursing home. No drugs, no long naps. I will *not* allow him to doze his days away, even though left to himself he'd do nothing else. I *will* bring him back to upright and engaged. For the eight remaining months of that first healing year, I devise stringent regimens to keep him alert and exercised. I take him to his therapies by subway instead of by taxi, forcing him to climb those challenging flights of stairs, and I forestall his falling when the train lurches by boldly claiming one of the seats reserved for the disabled. I insist, whenever possible, on walking to the library, the markets, the video store, the restaurants, stretching him to his limit, and once it's reached, I let him get a second wind in a park or a café before heading home. I remind him to *lead with the heel, not the toe* of his shuffling left foot and to *take long strides*, as Ilsa prescribes. I cajole or bully him into daily drawing sessions, having him sign an "agreement" for ten minutes of art a day. I lay out the materials, set the kitchen timer, and count it a success if he sits at the art table till the timer rings, even if he merely scribbles. Together we fill in the daily calendar and activities chart provided by the occupational therapist. In the evenings I turn on his favorite basketball teams and give him his earphones in the vain hope that, as in the past, he will watch the game alone and let me read. When that fails, I give in and watch with him.

The outpatient physical therapist, Frania Zins, who practices a subtle kind of body manipulation called the Feldenkrais Method, is reputed to be a genius at understanding the injured body. Recommended to us by a friend whose chronic pain she cured, Frania soon has Scott walking blocks at a time with less shuffling of his left foot and without the backache he's suffered since his fall. Analyzing his peculiar movements, the consequence not only of his injuries but of months of hospital-imposed immobility, Frania identifies his main problem area as his pelvis and devises an exercise that involves his smoothly rocking his pelvis forward and back ten times, first seated, then supine, which I add to his prescribed morning routine. He calls it *fucky-fucky*.

Too impaired to recognize its benefits, he resists all exercise, opening the first crack in my dedication. He will exercise only if I join him. Rather than begin the day in discord, I sit or lie beside him on the bed in my nightclothes, squeeze my shoulder blades together, lift my legs, and roll my pelvis alongside him. So it happens that one morning we progress seamlessly from fucky-fucky the exercise to making love.

This outcome takes me completely by surprise. I had assumed sex was over and frankly didn't mind. From the moment of Scott's miraculous survival and on through his gradual and partial recovery, his broken body had become to me paradoxically both more precious and less accessible, like some fragile treasure wrapped in tissue paper that one unwraps gingerly and rarely, for fear of damaging it. Sex, which over the years had been gradually diminishing as a frequent element in our life, seemed a risky frivolity, making this spontaneous eruption feel like a memory trip. Starting in 1950 in that Cleveland motel when we were seventeen and twenty, our sex was secret, fraught, and fast—no better or worse than could be expected, given our inexperience and the times. But by the 1980s, when Scott reappeared in my life, we were in our fifties, and the cultural upheavals of the 1960s and 1970s, including the "sexual revolution," had presumably taught everyone a thing or two. On one of his early visits to me in New York, after a long Italian lunch at the Grand Ticino (now gone), through which we had genially flirted as we sipped red wine and played at old-friends-getting-reacquainted, I invited him back to my empty apartment on Washington Square. The door had barely closed behind us before, right there in the entrance hall, he pressed one hand against the wall and the other into the small of my back to pull me toward him as he planted on my lips a kiss so much more ardent than I was prepared for by our conventional lunchtime banter, a kiss so unrestrained and stirring that it threw me completely off balance. I felt it in my knees and down to my toes. Who was this man? What did he expect of me? With that kiss I was on notice that whoever he was, he was not, as I had imagined, someone to toy or trifle with.

Not that I eschewed the pleasures of flirtation and conquest, which, before the women's movement, had been my exciting substitute for satisfying sex and, after the movement, became an entrée to and enhancement of my newly attainable sexual satisfaction. But I could see that he was too serious, too dear, and, as I quickly sensed, too vulnerable for any ordinary dalliance. This confused me. His combination of knockout good looks, Harvard education, and worldly accomplishment made him seem at first the sort of man who could lead an adversarial woman on a hard, challenging romp. But in an instant that kiss negated the outer trappings of alpha male and exposed him. It made me leery of starting something I might not know how to finish (though when I read him this passage he insists it was he who started something—which he never had any intention of finishing). Despite my misgivings, that afternoon we went straight from the entrance hall to my bed.

At that time, he and I lived in different sexual worlds: he, still stuck in the midwestern sexual culture of the 1950s; I, cavorting through the lush landscape opened up by the women's movement of the 1970s.

I had married and borne two children in the era before the movement began—an era marked by a double standard whereby wives were supposed to remain faithful even to blatantly unfaithful husbands. Not for that had I fled Ohio for New York. Once I discovered that my then-husband had begun an unbroken series of affairs shortly after the birth of our second child, I saw no reason to forgo the ecstasy erupting everywhere around me. Although older by a decade than the "liberated" youths of the counterculture, I looked no worse and had no less hunger than they had—plus, with my edge in experience, I had a knack they lacked. Then why let the new culture pass me by? At first I restricted my forays into that exciting world to the times when my husband was away philandering; then, as I became increasingly disillusioned with my marriage and emboldened by the powerful ideas of women's liberation, I claimed it for my own.

After I had spent years inhabiting my new persona and the movement had made me strong, Scott reentered my life from another age. I would not and could not step into a time machine back to the old ways just to make him comfortable, but neither could I risk embarrassing or humiliating this passionate dinosaur who so unexpectedly moved me. I call him dinosaur not because he was sexually aggressive—that had never been his style—but because, gentleman that he was, he seemed to consider sex a disrespectful imposition on a woman. That assumption may have had a certain validity in the 1950s, when sexual satisfaction was so unequally distributed and the consequences of transgression could be extreme, but by the 1980s it was a strange anachronism.

As we lay together in my bed that afternoon, he tried, as in our first affair, to spare me a long encounter, skipping the tender niceties of extended foreplay. And though I would never again stoop to faking an orgasm to soothe a male ego, I bowed to that supremely delicate organ by giving subtle instructions and taking care, as in the distant past, not to bruise it.

In those days of early 1980s backlash, I was still idealistic enough to believe that with patience and dedication, feminism could convert a good part of mankind to the principles of equality, one lover at a time. Scott, innocent and unreconstructed, was as eager a pupil as I could hope for. He embraced the feminist goal as his own. He readily agreed to my requirements for reaching orgasm: a few pulls on a joint to obliterate my self-consciousness, love of the clitoris, the right music, and plenty of time.

As a youth, I had never had an easy time with orgasm. I came of age in an era when foreplay was a moment's indulgence and sexual climax was often reserved for men. Always eager to please my partner and get it over with quickly, I learned to fake my orgasm as soon as I sensed that his was approaching. Like many women of my generation, I had no idea how transporting sex could be until I was in my thirties. (Susan Sontag, my exact contemporary, reports in a published excerpt from her journal that it wasn't until after she was a mother that she had her first orgasm.) Even after I became aware of the possibilities for women's sexual pleasure, and even under the best of circumstances, orgasm had always been chancy for me.

But with Scott, sex was different. He was so eager to please me that before long, I no longer needed to smoke a joint. Though our sex was not wild or dangerous or abandoned, it was always climactic and unembarrassed. Other lovers I'd had might have been more inventive, heart-stopping, and in tune with my own rhythms than he, but most of them fell into the category of "impossible"—that is, there were always reasons I couldn't trust them or otherwise want to be with them for long. Perhaps it was the very traits that disqualified them as mates that also made them sexually thrilling. In contrast, Scott's lovemaking was tender and absolutely dependable. Though at first it took a while to slow him down, he was the most considerate and attentive of lovers once he knew how to please me.

What had always been my toughest sexual hurdle, trusting my partner not to abandon me before I climaxed, did not apply with him, because I knew he would never abandon me and I felt I could trust him with my life.

Ah, the excesses of new passion! I remember the summer we rented a house together in Santa Fe, between my two teaching years in Boulder, when Scott and I were so besotted with each other that we actually considered having a child, though I was fifty-two, with menopause knocking, and he'd had a vasectomy (which he assured me was reversible). When I told my children, who had just graduated from college, what we were considering, Polly gave us her blessing because, she said, despite our years, if anything happened to us, she would be able to raise the child, and her brother soon concurred.

But except in those courtship days, when we made love every single chance we could, and on through our first few years of living together, when we dedicated those Tuesday afternoons to romance, sex was more an adjunct, an ecstasy, a deepening, than the engine of our intimacy.

Then, two years after our wedding (in our loft, with a feminist judge officiating, witnessed by half a dozen friends, our children, and my elderly parents, whom Scott adopted as his own) and three months before I turned sixty, Scott collapsed with an aortic aneurysm and our entire love life changed. Acutely aware of what I feared to lose if he didn't survive, I didn't care one bit that during the subsequent year of gradual healing his sex urge diminished drastically. So did mine. We both understood that some things are more important than others.

After Scott entered his seventies, though we continued to make plenty of time for dancing on our private dance floor, our sex dropped off to perhaps once or twice a month. Nothing we officially acknowledged, but the fact that we kept postponing it meant that neither of us craved more. And why should we? We knew we were connected by something deeper and more enduring than the sexual, combining companionship, respect, loyalty, mutual support, comfort, and understanding into a tranquil love that seemed only to increase with the years, with or without sex. So it's no surprise that after Scott's accident we barely ever mentioned it. Yet under the impetus of Frania's exercises, in our sudden crisis, sex came out of retirement to reinfuse our lives.

As with fucky-fucky, so with most everything we do together. My passionate purpose is to stimulate his brain and help him heal, while for him, unable for the most part to lay down new memories, whatever we do must be for its own sake. "Living in the moment" is not a goal for him, but the only available option, the default position.

❦

Until Scott's fall, I divided experience into two distinct kinds, both of which any satisfying life depends upon: the first, the pleasurable transitory experience, often sensual, that vanishes with the night; and the second, the kind of stable, future-oriented experience you build upon—work accomplished, knowledge accumulated, habit inculcated, skills expanded, resources conserved. But at some point in a long life the future begins to seem increasingly illusory, or at least a bad bet. Keep accumulating knowledge, conserving your eyesight and your money—for what? At that point it may be time to forget about self-improvement and start to read only what grabs you; ignore the calories and pig out; stay up listening to music half the night; take in a movie in the afternoon.

I had begun to brood on this dilemma back when we entered our seventies, wondering if the time hadn't come to start rebalancing our accounts by turning our sights from the future

to the present and ourselves from ants to grasshoppers, who—
face it—probably have more fun. Still addicted to hope, which
always faces forward, and with no diminishment in energy despite my age, I knew it might take considerable effort to pull off
such a change, but I was ready to give it a try. Then, with
Scott's fall, the long-standing relationship between present and
future in our lives abruptly collapsed. Whereas I, fixated on
healing him, examined minutely everything he said or did for
its bearing on his future recovery, he, ignorant of the day, the
month, the season, the year, and unable to remember the recent
past or think ahead to the next moment, could conceive of
nothing but the immediate present. Which meant that the kind
of experience he had spent his life accumulating in order to
expand his capacities was now impossible for him, just as abandoning myself to the pleasures of the moment became impossible for me. (Dancing, for example, which I'd always done for
the sheer expressive joy of it, became a means of building up
his strength.) Instead of each of us partaking of both kinds of
experience, after the traumas of the summer we divided them
between us, until now we inhabit disparate time frames, he the
present, I the future, permanently out of sync, coming together
only to rendezvous in our common past.

"What traumas?" he asks, puzzled, after I read him this.
    "You know—your fall."
    "I fell? Where?"
    "At the nubble. From the balcony in the studio."
    "Oh, that. Don't bring that up again. What a stupid thing
to do!"
    "It was an accident!"
    "A stupid accident."
    To change the subject I ask him if he minds my writing
about our sex life.
    "Of course not. Why would I mind?"

"Some people might think it's too private to put in a book."

"You know I love what you write. I trust you completely. Anyway, it's all true, isn't it?"

"Yes, but for others to read about?"

"Absolutely! I want everything you write, about us or not about us, to be out in the world. You know that's the truth from my inner heart."

Yes I do.

One day, arriving early at Rusk for his cognitive therapy session, to kill time I take him down to the inpatient floors to show off how far he's come. He greets each of his former therapists and nurses with outstretched hand, as if he actually recognized them: "Hello. So good to see you. How have you been?" They are amazed by how confidently he walks, how normal he appears. The last time they saw him, his walking distance was measured in feet, not blocks, he was afflicted with fluent aphasia, and he believed the hospital was a hotel, a corporate headquarters, a sports arena, a prison. Now his speech is back to normal and he can walk ten blocks (half a mile) before he's undone by fatigue. They pass him from one to another, like a living miracle, while I gloat over his achievements—which I take as personally as any page well written or complex subject understood. *Not your standard seventy-five-year-old,* I remember proudly.

In the wake of his progress, my ambitions for him expand to fill every crack. To our repertory I soon add concerts, plays, dance events, and whichever museums provide wheelchairs— the same pleasures as before his fall, but for me with the heightened purpose of healing him. At night we watch more movies than I'd have chosen to see in a lifetime. I'd much prefer to read, but he refuses to watch unless I join him, on threat of going straight to sleep, which would risk his rising at dawn and rousing me with him. Instead I watch with him, then slip out of bed to read after he's asleep, my only respite from his care. *Compromise* and *accommodation*, of which he was once a master, have now become my bywords.

At the Museum of Modern Art, at the crowded Redon exhibit, he invokes his "manhood" to insist that part of the time *I* ride in the wheelchair, allowing *him* to push *me*. It's absurd! The chair will be too heavy for him, and there's nothing wrong with me. But since his inability to reason renders my arguments useless, to humor him I give in. Our luck, as soon as I'm in the wheelchair, a woman from a seminar I attend stops to chat with us, pretending that nothing is strange—for which I'm grateful, since I'm too embarrassed to explain. Is that pity in her voice? Is she patronizing me? Does she see through our pretense? The next time we visit a museum I adamantly hold my ground: I will push, he will ride —period! Luckily too, since I doubt he'd be strong enough to hold back the wheelchair on the continuous downhill six-story ramp that is the Guggenheim. (I'm reminded of Aesop's fable of the man, his son, and the donkey. For the entire journey, for fear of what people will say, the father and son keep switching off who rides and who walks, until they both wind up carrying the donkey. The moral: forget about others' opinions and do what you must.)

Thus, reluctantly, do I become a tyrant. I tell him when to ride and when to stand, when to sleep and when to wake, what to wear and how to dress, which mental and physical exercises to perform, what and when to eat, how much water to drink with his medicines, which medicines, how to brush and floss his teeth, when to sit on the toilet. I instruct him on how to walk and how far, where and when we may rest, which way to turn, what door to enter, what key to use, when he may and may not go out. I tell him which pens to draw with, which dishes to use, which sofa to lie on. I try to couch my orders in gentle language. Knowing he won't remember what he asked for, "later" becomes my fallback answer to his requests, as "now" is the time frame in which I issue mine. In the end I have no choice but to be the boss—as he frequently points out.

On bad days, frustrated by the confusion that makes him unable to comply with my wishes, he loses it and yells—as much at himself as at me. Sometimes when I'm impatient with his mistakes, as when he puts his pants on backward or resets the table as soon as we've finished clearing off the dirty dishes, he's so disheartened by his failures that he vows to shoot himself. When he stalks through the loft yelling and cursing, both of us feel battered and oppressed, though afterward he regrets losing his control, as I sometimes regret having to enforce mine.

His outbursts are completely new to me. Before his accident, his style of conflict was to go silent. Which surprised me, because early on, both his daughter and his former secretary warned me about his temper. Donna, his secretary, spoke to me about it at our first meeting. Eager for the people in his life to know each other, Scott had invited us both to lunch at Sammy's, a popular restaurant in downtown Cleveland, during one of my trips to visit my parents. When he left the table to pay the check, Donna leaned over to tell me that though she had never had a better boss than Scott, she thought it her duty to warn me about a side of him she was pretty sure I hadn't seen. For instance, several months earlier he had slammed down the phone so hard it had broken, and once, she had found her predecessor crying in the ladies' room because of the way he had spoken to her, though she assured me he had never once raised his voice to *her*. "He knows if he ever pulled that on me, I'd quit."

Though my experience of Scott was nothing like hers, in the following months I brooded over Donna's cautionary words, remembered them as he and I moved steadily closer to living together. But in the end, having personally seen no evidence of his hot temper (on the contrary, our one and only fight during our courtship, over who should pack up the car when we left Santa Fe for Boulder, ended not in shouting but in tears over the frightening prospect of splitting up), I chose to ignore her warning and risk it. And during the twenty years we were together before his fall, so powerful is inhibition—or character, or will—that even though I couldn't always control my anger, as far as I recall he never once directly aimed his at me. The alternative mode of conflict called "passive aggressive" was in Scott's case far more passive than aggressive. Even now, his outbursts pass quickly because he forgets them in a moment, and rather than smolder with resentment, he thanks me for "sticking by" him.

Since well before his accident we had been looking forward to what promised to be a spectacular New York City art event, Christo and Jeanne-Claude's Central Park Gates, an installation of thousands of large saffron-colored cloth panels hung from seventy-five hundred squared arches spaced along twenty-three miles of footpaths in Central Park. By the time it opened on February 12, 2005, there had been tremendous anticipation by the public and hoopla in the press. A quarter century and millions of dollars in the making, this colossal installation was scheduled to remain up for only sixteen days, after which it would be dismantled and recycled.

"Do you want to see the Christo Gates?" I ask Scott, unsure if he'll know what I'm talking about.

"Of course I do," he replies without hesitation.

Even though there's snow on the ground, three days later,

on a cold, sparkling afternoon during the first week of the Gates, I bundle him up in his warmest coat and his safest hiking boots and we take the A train to Columbus Circle at Fifty-ninth Street, our nearest access to Central Park.

Hawkers, vendors, and buskers fill the park's entrance area, making it hard to walk—the very conditions that can quickly produce an "overload" in Scott's slow and halting brain. As he grumbles about the hullabaloo, I fear the whole excursion may be a bust. But when we finally get past the congestion into the park itself and begin our walk among the jaunty orange flags, calm takes over, and he joins in the celebratory mood of the other strollers—people of every sort and style who smile cheerfully, greeting one another as if we were all guests at a festive party instead of self-protective New Yorkers. To crises like subway strikes, blizzards, and blackouts, I now add pleasure and art for bringing out the affable best in all of us.

"Isn't it enchanting?" Scott exclaims again and again as we meander along, sometimes tipping his hat to oncoming strollers, despite the cold. "It's like a Buddhist parade!" he cries, waving at the saffron panels, and when we pause to look down on the park from a high point, he remarks that it looks like a brilliant golden river winding its way uptown. He walks without his usual post-accident fear of falling, reaching up to touch the panels, smiling at strangers, until he tires, at which point we simply sit on one of the many benches lining the paths until the cold sinks in and he's ready to walk again. An hour passes before he abruptly announces that it's time to go home.

Twice more we return to the Gates—Scott because he wants to see them again, I because I want to witness his pleasure. Unlike movies or meals or visits with friends, which he forgets the moment they're over, miraculously he remembers the Gates, first for days, then weeks, and eventually for years. Is this because, having anticipated them before the accident, he's

able to slot them into old memory rather than new? Or because of something in the artistic experience itself? Or simply
as another of the unfathomable mysteries of his condition?

In the late afternoons, as he lies in front of the window staring
out, oblivious of his accident and filled with happiness—at the
blue sky, at so much "face time" with me, at the beauty of our
loft—I know his happiness is true, know that those who assume
we're in mourning for our former life are wrong. Daily he
takes my hand to proclaim how lucky we are, and I remember
that in the early days of our courtship, whenever his brain was
impaired by too much alcohol, he was a happy drunk, never
belligerent or contentious or brooding, foolish perhaps but always upbeat and affectionate—as he is still. This part of his nature is probably so deeply wired in his brain as to have escaped
damage. Like me, he rejects unhappiness as counterproductive.
To both of us, action and accommodation are always preferable
to passivity or despair, which can only prolong the pain. If all
else fails we'll use our tragedy for making art. ("All sorrows can
be borne if you put them into a story," wrote Isak Dinesen.)
Deep down, we're ready to wait out the bad until the good returns, however long it takes.

Our shorthand for this tenacious optimism, which some
consider temperament, others self-delusion or denial, and still
others a gift, is the language of luck—which we continually
manufacture by our stubborn resistance to viewing our lives as
other than blessed.

For example, unaware of his accident, Scott attributes his
failed memory and aching back not to one of life's arbitrary
blows, but to normal aging, which he accepts and even cele-
brates as "better than the alternative." (So much for that *No, I
don't think so. No.*) "Aren't we lucky to be growing old together?" he asks.

At first I dismiss the idea that his age has anything to do with his condition. A calamitous mishap like his could occur to anyone at any time and just happened to tear into our lives in our seventies. Man falls off balcony, suffers traumatic injuries, changes irrevocably. But the more I think about it, the less sure I am. Can it be because of his age that the fall occurred that summer and none of the previous fifteen summers when he slept on that balcony and didn't fall? Old people famously fall. Though it's his injury, not his age that has destroyed his memory, age can't be entirely ruled out. He may have been straight and strong going into that summer, but he came out of it bent, slow, and confused, like many another man his age. At Rusk, whenever I asked about his prognosis, the doctors would hedge their answers by invoking his advancing years. At the time, I couldn't understand why, but since then my studies have taught me that an aging brain is more vulnerable to decline than a young one, even without a disastrous fall, and that a blow to the head at any age can precipitate future dementia.

The truth is, until the accident I never thought of either of us as *old*, an adjective that might apply to other people in their seventies, especially those I read about in novels or obituaries, but not to us. We didn't act old, didn't look old (at least not to each other), didn't think old or feel old. True, ever since his aneurysm Scott's memory had been fading, but not so much that I couldn't fill in for him whatever was missing. We went on about our lives as always, he off each morning to his studio and I to my writing desk—not without, to be sure, some of the usual vicissitudes of septuagenarian life, annoying memory lapses, thinning hair, bones getting fragile, new sags and wrinkles unexpectedly appearing. And we had taken care to put our affairs in order—made our wills, advised our children of our wishes, rationalized our financial accounts. But in truth, we had first made wills when we were young, when our children were born. And the wrinkles and lapses of memory too had begun in our youth and accompanied us on every step of the way, along with our share of broken bones and progressive hair loss—all unremarkable, ubiquitous. Then out of the blue this trauma, and (even though the beds on either side of Scott in the ICU were occupied by reckless or diseased youths) we are suddenly plunged into old age.

"Can you believe how old we've gotten?" he exclaims as he rests on our bed while I dress.

"I know. It's hard to believe."

"But actually, I'm finding it rather enjoyable, aren't you?"

"Right!" I laugh. "No more of that restless striving or vain ambition."

"And we know so much by now," says the man who knows so little.

I give myself a little shake. If he, with his disabling deficits, can hold fast to his lifelong habit of contentment, then I, without them, must find it in me to master sorrow and do the same.

FIVE

Thriller

The summer I turned fourteen, I spent a month at the Lake Erie resort town of Cedar Point with a friend whose parents ran a food concession on the boardwalk, which boasted the highest roller coaster in Ohio. It was called the Thriller, and I fell in love with it. I hung around it so much that the daytime manager, seeing my passion, eventually allowed me to ride for free in the mornings, when there weren't many customers. One day I decided to see how many consecutive rides I could clock without stopping and rode for two and a half hours straight. Even so, the thrill of the slow clank to the top followed by the heart-stopping plunge to the bottom continued unabated.

After I had children of my own, my reckless daring gradually drained out of me until they could not induce me to accompany them on the big rides, and then not on the small ones either, until finally I swore off all of them—a not uncommon side effect of responsibility. Now I wonder if my youthful fearlessness and love of danger didn't somehow prepare me to deal with Scott's accident and its aftermath, a similar extreme alternation of anticipation, tension, terror, and relief. With Scott himself incapable of either hope or dread, I took the ride for us both, clutching the sides, holding my breath, screaming as we fell, hanging on for dear life, bracing for the next slow uphill climb.

On the night of the accident, that precipitous plunge, I wept torrents. Not as I looked down from the sleeping loft to the floor below where my beloved lay broken, but later, in the tiny windowless waiting room of the hospital ER, where I hung on the edge awaiting the doctor's verdict. The tears wouldn't stop. However, during Scott's weeks in the ICU, as the clicking chains and squeaky gears carried us slowly upward toward the successive peaks, where he would be roused from his drug-induced coma, or mechanically lifted from bed and lowered into a chair, or taken off the respirator, or discharged home, my adrenaline-charged anticipation kept me hopeful and dry-eyed. On the Thriller, the exhilarating buildup of anticipation followed by alternating terror at the imminent peril and relief at having momentarily survived it kept me in a state of hermetic equilibrium, which didn't abate until the moment I returned, wobbly and off balance, to terra firma. Just so, every time I left the enclosed world of Scott's accident for the world outside, my precarious stability broke down, opening the floodgates again.

Everyone who cared about us said it was essential for me to return to the world and reclaim my life, as if it were something important I had temporarily parked in a checkroom. In principle I agreed it would be a good thing to try, and to accomplish this I compiled a list of potential Scott Watchers, mostly students whom I reached through a posting on an NYU website and interviewed as carefully as if I were leaving them with my newborn. Their job, I said, would be to spend the evening with Scott watching a movie or a game on TV while I went out—to one of the monthly meetings or seminars I had attended regularly before the accident, or to meet a friend for dinner (after I'd given Scott his)—as if I were still the engaged writer, activist, friend. But usually an evening out had the opposite of the desired effect, making me feel less like a participant than like an onlooker or, worse, a pretender. The sympathetic concern of friends only exacerbated my sense of alienation. "Are you taking care of yourself?" "Are you able to work?" asked one after another of those who work, write, organize, teach, and travel abroad during their sabbaticals and vacations, oblivious of what lies in store for them. As the months slipped by, I felt the distance between me and the world expanding, like continents adrift.

❦

My friend Sarah, a writer and retired psychology professor whom I haven't seen since Scott's fall nearly a year ago, is visiting from the West Coast. For the first time, I dare to leave him during daytime hours in order to have lunch with her, hiring my most reliable Scott Watcher to replace me.

This afternoon will be nothing like those evening dates I force myself to make because I think they're good for me but which often leave me disturbed or shaken. Today I haven't a trace of ambivalence; I've been counting the days. Sarah—whose husband, George, at eighty-nine suffers from age-related memory impairment (ARMI)—is the only friend I have who also lives with a demented mate. Comparing notes with her by phone always helps me think about my situation more clearly; it's a comfort to confess my secret thoughts and deeds to someone who knows firsthand what it's like. Since I can't leave Scott alone in order to attend one of the caregivers' support groups the doctors recommend, I can hardly wait to spend an entire afternoon face-to-face with Sarah—eighty, experienced, and wise.

At noon she meets me at our loft. While I get my coat she talks to Scott. To me, he appears to be making a tolerably normal impression—if not recognizing Sarah, then successfully faking it, inquiring about her husband, and even managing to introduce the Scott Watcher by fudging the names. So I'm taken aback when, as soon as the door closes behind us, Sarah shakes her head and says, "I could never do what you're doing."

"What do you mean?"

"I mean if George were as bad off as Scott, I couldn't take care of him the way you do. I couldn't do it."

I don't believe her. "Of course you could if you had to. You'd have no choice."

"No," she says emphatically as we exit the building and head north, "I couldn't. I wouldn't. I wouldn't give over my life the way you do. I wouldn't be able to."

I hope Sarah's reaction isn't just another version of the response of certain friends who think I should arrange for his care and get on with my life, as if his self had perished and he could be reduced to his disabilities—or of those who view me as incomprehensibly long-suffering, self-sacrificing, saintly, a caricature that's hardly an unmitigated compliment. For every friend who admires my devotion to my calling, another is indignant, perhaps terrified of finding herself in my place. "Are you trying to be some kind of hero or something, or is this just *love*?" asked one friend bluntly. "Your patience and forbearance are incredible," e-mailed another; and I was told by a mutual friend that another friend considers my caring for Scott "not a virtue but a vice." ("But why?" I asked. "Apparently she thinks you're being untrue to yourself.") As if I had a choice! Yes, it's a drag to take care of him, I want to say, just as it's often a drag to take care of your children, but you do it for love. Instead I reply to all of them: in my circumstances you'd do the same.

Still, I recognize that my testy response might be excessive, particularly since there was a time when I too might have viewed a calling such as mine with suspicion. Once I became aware of the ubiquitous expectations of female sacrifice in the name of service, I too might have called for principled resis-

tance in the name of justice. And not only on principle: I confess that if it had been my previous husband instead of Scott
who had fallen, I might have been tempted to bolt at the first
exit. Ever leery of giving my heart away, thinking it a dangerous folly even in marriage, I always reserved for myself the tra-
ditionally male prerogative to cut and run. As a girl, then a
woman, I knew I had too little power to risk the handicap that
unprotected love would impose, preferring the advantage con-
ferred by a cavalier attitude toward each escapade. Though from
puberty onward I was usually coupled, sometimes, feeling the
need to move on, I exercised my right to disappear on a lover,
pulling off my escape with a sense of relief that verged on triumph—the more so because the prospect of being alone was
always scary to me until I went off to live alone on an island
the summer I turned fifty and taught myself to survive. My
conception of love as "free" released me from any obligation to
stick around, much less to sacrifice.

All this changed for me one Friday, two years after our
wedding, when Scott collapsed with his aortic aneurysm. We
were living in Honolulu, where I was a visiting professor at the
University of Hawaii. That day he was working in the art department's foundry, casting a new piece of sculpture. After he
lowered an extremely heavy mold filled with molten bronze
into a cooling vat, he suddenly crumpled to the floor.

The English department secretary summoned me out of my
class to take a phone call in her office. "It's the hospital," she
whispered. "An emergency." My hands were already shaking as
I picked up the phone. A doctor informed me that Scott was
about to undergo emergency heart surgery and that I must get
to the hospital immediately to sign releases.

To cut open his heart? I thought of all the exposés of itchy-
fingered surgeons performing unnecessary operations. Who was
this doctor proposing to put a knife in that precious heart?

"Can't we get a second opinion?" said my mother's voice through my lips.

"I'm afraid there's no time for a second opinion. We need to operate immediately."

"And if you don't?"

"Your husband may die in the next several hours."

Die!

"May I talk to him?"

Scott's voice, shaky but insistent, came on the phone. "Just come," he said. "Hurry."

I had never heard him speak so urgently; insistence was not his style. Tears blinded me as I took down directions to the ICU of a provincial hospital whose name I didn't recognize, staffed by doctors I'd never heard of. I looked at the clock. The madness of Honolulu rush hour had already begun; how would I get there without losing my way in this foreign city?

I asked the secretary to dismiss my class for me and ran to the parking lot. Somehow I managed to find my car keys, start the car. Despite my fear of driving, which came from living for three decades in Manhattan without a car, and my miserable sense of direction, I did not get lost. When I arrived at the ICU, Scott insisted from his bed, with his usual aplomb, that before we permitted anyone to operate on his heart, we needed another—a trusted—opinion. I agreed. But whose? Then I remembered. A renowned professor of cardiology at the University of Connecticut, author of a standard cardiology textbook and onetime officer of the American Heart Association, happened to be my first cousin. And though it was years since we had spoken and it was already midnight in Connecticut, I found my cousin's number and called it. Relief flooded through me when his wife answered sleepily, "Just a minute, here's Arnie." My cousin interrogated the surgical team about their credentials, diagnosis, intentions, and equipment before—

with calming reassurances—he gave his approval and told me to sign.

While Scott was being prepped for surgery, I sat alone in a waiting room until a nurse led me onto a corridor where his gurney would pass by en route to the operating room. Moments later he arrived. He took my hand and, looking gravely into my eyes, said those words that would change everything for me: "Whatever happens to me, I want you to know that you were truly loved." Then he was wheeled down the hall and disappeared.

Until that day I had never imagined the possibility of his dying. Nor how it would devastate me. We thought of our marriage as an experimental union of two autonomous souls. We prided ourselves on keeping our finances separate and spending our summers apart. After living together for years without benefit of wedlock, why we finally decided to turn the key locking us into legal marriage was still a mystery, though neither of us had a single qualm. We sometimes said glibly that we did it for the taxes and insurance, but we both secretly knew that was a lie. Now, as he delivered the message he had chosen as his parting words to me, perhaps his last words on earth, our vaunted separateness was exposed as a sham. I recognized in that moment that he was as much a part of me as my limbs, and that given the chance, I would willingly renounce my independent life to restore his.

I returned to the waiting room and gave way to a convulsion of tears. The memory of that goodbye, playing over and over in my mind, kept me weeping, even after a large family from Tonga, whose father/uncle/brother/grandfather was having heart surgery at the same time as Scott, filled up the room. I sat quietly in a corner trying to be unobtrusive, but the tears just kept coming.

There were eight or nine Tongans, all huge, ranging from children to elderly, filling the small room with their imposing size and the lilting strains of their language. I recognized it from the Tongan church in Honolulu that Scott and I sometimes attended on Sunday mornings for the celestial choral music. Eventually they noticed me weeping in the corner. A very large woman in her forties, with a wide, brown, kindly face and a spray of gardenias in her waistlong hair, came over to me and with one sweep of her muscular arm raised me up out of my chair and enfolded me in a fragrant embrace. Then one by one the entire family lined up to hug me. In minimal English supplemented by sign language they asked about Scott and told me about their father. They were dismayed that I was alone, that I had no family to turn to. I tried to explain that it was the middle of the night on the mainland, and even if I called someone, what good would it do? No one would be able to come. Our families were different from theirs. Scott was an only child and his parents were dead; my only brother had recently died and my parents were too old to travel; my children, thousands of miles away, had busy lives we wouldn't think of interrupting; and Scott's daughter was pregnant and forbidden to fly.

The Tongans just shook their heads in pity. For the few hours we were together in the hospital, they welcomed me as one of their own, sharing their bagfuls of food—fruit, chicken, chips, sodas, sweet cakes—which they kept replenishing from outside. I was so comforted by their warmth and generosity that when they left a few hours later, I felt bereft. In their place, my tears returned to keep me company as I sat in my corner, alone again, with nothing to distract me from the knowledge that Scott could die at any moment, and then how would I be able to live?

Around dawn the surgeon came into the waiting room to inform me that he had sewn into Scott's heart a "valved conduit"—a mechanical valve with a new section of aorta attached—to replace his damaged tissue. It took them seven hours because, after discovering Scott's malformed valve once they opened him up, they had to contact all the hospitals in town to find the kind of valve they needed to repair his heart.

It was May, the end of the academic year. The plumeria trees that lined the path from the street to our house were in full blossom, and the garden and terrace had never smelled more fragrant. Ripe papayas and mangoes I'd had no time to pick from our fecund trees lay rotting on the ground. Fortunately, by the time I brought Scott home from the hospital I had only two more classes to teach, plus exams, leaving me free to devote myself entirely to him. Ignorant of how to nurse him, I improvised. As prescribed, I took him walking down the hill in front of our house, timing him for two minutes, then three minutes, then five, each time running back for the car to drive him up the hill again—trying to get him in shape for the arduous trip back to New York. Even as I packed up a year's worth of stuff to ship home, I hovered over him, trying to get him to eat (he was all bones), walk, climb stairs, heal. And all the time, whether we were in bed or seated at the table or walking on the street, I could hear his new valve clicking away inside his chest, proclaiming the miracle of his survival and summoning me to my task. With his parting words emblazoned in my mind, the self-protective resistance I'd cultivated all my life melted away as I embraced instead devotion.

Now I think of that time in Hawaii as training and preparation for harder times to come. For now.

As Sarah and I continue our walk together, I assume her feelings for George are something like mine for Scott. Her second husband, he encouraged and supported her work as Scott did mine. He raised her child as his own, he was her best friend and great love, and like us they've been together for decades. So why is she saying that in my place she wouldn't do for George what I do for Scott?

We're walking without a destination, walking for the pleasure of walking with no particular restaurant in mind. It's an
unseasonably mild afternoon, sunny with just the right whisper
of breeze, one of those days that makes New York the best
walking city in the world. On this day even the traffic seems
restrained.

"I don't believe you," I say. "You'd feel responsible for him
and do what you have to do. As you do now."

"Oh but that's very different. Right now I'm visiting here
in New York and George is back home in Seattle, alone.
Friends look in on him in the evenings, but he can still manage
by himself. Not like Scott."

"Yes, but if he got worse you'd adapt to it."

When we stop for a light she turns to me to make her
point. "I know I have only a limited time left, and I want to
live out my last years as fully as I can. George and I decided
long ago that if we ever reached a point where we couldn't take
care of ourselves, we wouldn't ask it of each other."

"What would you do, then—put him in a nursing home?"

"I'd hire someone else to care for him and just live my life."

I am shocked. Not only by her declaration (which I don't
believe, no matter what she says) but by her view of my situation. I hadn't thought of it as all that terrible. It has plenty of
problems and bad moments, yes, but it's also full of purpose and
satisfactions, not least that of rising to the challenge. Hardly so
intolerable that I must try to escape it—an idea so alien I've
barely even fantasized about it. (On the contrary, what fantasies
I have are not about escaping, but about holding fast. I focus on
what will become of him should something happen to me—
though any plans I may make will be moot, since his daughter,
his legal next of kin, will be in charge once I'm gone, and my
wishes will be irrelevant.)

Now, through Sarah's eyes, I become aware that the life I'm

living is neither inevitable nor necessary: I actually have choices. And as we stroll through the stimulating streets on my first free walk since bringing Scott home, engaged in intimate, engrossing conversation that I had somehow forgotten could happen, I am stabbed by an awareness of all I've lost. To walk with my head up and my eyes free, without having to guide Scott slowly through traffic or direct him to lead with his left heel not his toe; to walk without clock or duty tugging me back; to stride aimlessly through my extended neighborhood with the bracing breeze riffling my hair and no purpose other than to exchange ideas with my friend and eventually find a pleasing restaurant—to be suddenly, recklessly free for the first time in a year—feels like bliss.

Afterward, exactly as high as my spirit has soared, it crashes to earth when I remember that giddy sense of freedom and how quickly it was punctured by Sarah's sobering words. Her stark view of my predicament has shocked me into seeing the shape my life has assumed and the magnitude of my loss: my writing is finished, our marriage is utterly unequal, and the world that was once my world has become unreal to me. All the passions, principles, and hard-won habits I built up over a lifetime have been undermined and overturned until, now, the writer whose work requires solitude is never alone; the adventurer seeking experience is tied to one spot; the intellectual jouster can no longer exchange ideas; the book lover can hardly ever read; the political activist must abandon the battlefield; the feminist devotee of equality is a one-way caregiver to someone deeply dependent.

In the following days I find myself crying whenever I'm alone, suddenly plagued by cold sores and insomnia, wondering if I'm losing my mind.

On Sunday, when my daughter comes to visit, the moment I greet her at the elevator (after daring to leave Scott alone in the loft while I dash down the hall), I burst into tears.

"What is it, Mom?"

"I think I may be having a nervous breakdown," I say sheepishly, trying to smile. I recount my conversation with Sarah, then blurt out despite myself, "I have no life."

Polly stops us in the hall and hugs me. "You've got to get some help, Mom. You can't go on doing this all by yourself."

We are almost at the door to our loft, where Scott is waiting. No time to say any more. But I know she's right; know that she, Sarah, Linda, Ann—all my good friends whose similar advice I've usually dismissed with righteous pride—see what I haven't been able to see: I can no longer do this alone.

I wipe my eyes and open the door.

"Oh there you are! At last! I thought I'd lost you!"

"Look, Scott. Polly's here."

The gracious host shuffles toward us and enfolds her in his arms.

What am I to do? Unless something changes drastically, I fear I will sink. Yet such are the mysteries of the brain that even as my crisis deepens, Scott's present condition, in the late summer of 2005, after the one-year anniversary of his accident has come and gone, seems to have stabilized.

Physically, he's much improved. He sleeps soundly every night. He eats with gusto and appreciation whatever I serve him, though choosing a menu is beyond him. His speech is fluent. With encouragement, he can now walk, albeit slowly, for three-quarters of a mile before fatigue cuts him down. He is reasserting his will: on a recent walk home from brunch at our favorite café, Rafaella's, when I prompted him (as always) to lead with the heel of his left foot, this time he replied, "I'll do no such thing! I refuse to be bullied about by the point guard of the feminist movement!"

Emotionally, he's more responsive, frequently moved to tears by music and sad stories. He overflows with spontaneous expressions of love and gratitude. The flip side of this common TBI trait "disinhibition" is that he is also easily frustrated and quick to feel rebuffed, to which he responds, as he never did before his fall, by cursing, shouting, slamming doors, throwing things—though when the spell passes a moment later and his deep-seated gentleness returns, he is also quick to apologize. "I'm just a blustering bastard. Can you ever forgive me?"

With hardly any improvement in his severely damaged short-term memory, he still can't recall having seen a film once it's over, much less follow a plot. But while he's watching, the movies engage him so completely that our bedroom resembles the cheering section at a sports event: "Take the offer, Humphrey!" he shouts at the screen. "Put your arm around her, Dumbo!" "I hope the doorman slugs him." "Oh come on, cut the malarkey." "You're on the wrong team, buster." Sometimes he indignantly tries to direct: "Get your ass off the stage!" Or, when the violins soar, "How dare you throw music around that way!" and to the scary tremolo of a film noir score, "That's enough music late at night out in the middle of nowhere."

Even if he can't figure out how to work the door buzzer to admit visitors, his social skills are intact, enabling him to ask the right questions, seem to listen to the answers, and show concern for the comfort of our guests. He can fake a conversation so well that it takes a long time for someone not in the know to realize anything is wrong with him. In a restaurant, even as I worry that he'll get lost coming back from the men's room, he interacts with the waiters so normally that they defer to him and hand him the check. He keeps our friends laughing with his playful rejoinders and amusing remarks. "Don't get too close to the snapdragons or they'll bite your fingers," he warns Ilsa. "You're stuck between a skillet and a hot plate," he remarks to Linda, inventively conflating *caught between a rock and a hard place*, and *going from frying pan to fire*. When Polly and her husband, Andrew, come to dinner, the minute we're finished eating Scott heads for the sofa, saying, "Please excuse me, I'm going to my contemplation couch. You're all welcome to join me if you like." Shortly afterward he calls out sweetly, "Yoo-hoo, I'm taking visitors now," and when we are slow to leave the table, he threatens to lodge a complaint with the Marriage Bureau.

Seated beside him a few minutes later, Polly scribbles down his words in her notebook while I look on, lamenting that I can never remember his best remarks.

"You have to write them in your diary as they occur," she says.

"I don't have a diary."

"That's because she has a dairy," pipes up Scott.

I know that substituting similar-sounding words is a symptom of aphasia, but his remark is still funny in a goofy sort of way. When we start to laugh he adds, "Because I gave her a cow," and he basks in our delight. "For Easter," he continues, stringing it out. "Come around next year and we'll have another animal." By now hilarity has overcome us all. He is clearly tickled to be the cause of it, but having lost all sense of absurdity—perhaps because to him everything verges on the absurd—he isn't sure why.

Still, he is more observant and alert than he was even a few months ago. He's good at telling time and reading the thermometer on our windowsill. His attention span has increased enough for him to once again mark up *The New Yorker*'s art gallery listings with asterisks and underlines—though as soon as we get to a gallery, he's ready to leave. Things that were lost on him since his fall—like the taxi meter, our wind sock (an American flag visible from our window that tells us which way the wind is blowing), an occasional news item on NPR—have begun to register. He again recognizes the president's voice and bristles when he hears it.

As with most TBI victims, however, his smarts and savvy have deserted him, and whether they will ever return would be futile to guess. "May I ask you a question?" he ventures hesitantly after hearing a radio report of renewed Israeli-Hezbollah violence. "Is it possible for me to join the Israeli army?" He can't originate an activity on his own or make a decision; indeed, all the crucial functions of the frontal cortex—initiating, organizing, and executing a plan; problem solving, reasoning, elaboration of thought, and all the higher cognitive functions that are the glory of our species; as well as the "gatekeeper" functions of judgment and inhibition—are now beyond his reach. Without them he can't begin to make art on his own. Nevertheless, if I issue instructions in the simplest form, one step at a time, he can again perform certain tasks he routinely did before his fall, like set the table, sort the laundry, put the trash down the chute, hang up the coats, pass the hors d'oeuvres.

He's showing more concern for me. Understanding my need to read (which his constant interruptions preclude), he comes up with a generous if loopy proposal. "I've got a good idea. I'll Scott Watch tonight so you can read. Would you like that?" Increasingly he asks: "Are we all right?" "Are you reasonably content with our life together?" "Do you know that all I want to do is keep you happy?" Even the disinhibition that leads to his shouting obscenities at me is sometimes tempered by restraint: when I ask why he's swearing at me, he says, "I'm not swearing at you, I'm just practicing in case I need to swear at you later."

It's clear that behind his foggy confusion and despite his disabling incapacities, Scott's self remains stubbornly intact. Not only has he daily stretches of lucidity, calm, and sweetness, lasting anywhere from moments to hours, when he seems himself again, able to discuss a familiar subject with a bit of clarity before reverting to his now customary muddle, but the enduring combination of traits that always distinguished his self from another's—his sunny optimism and charm, his aesthetic passion, his deep-rooted modesty, sincerity, courtesy, and generosity of spirit, as well as his diffidence and reserve—keep breaking through the fog.

Yet for all his continuities and improvements, he is still utterly dependent. He still finds the TV remote, a computer, a telephone menu, the building intercom, the stove, the locks on our door, and his key ring too flush with choices to operate. Sometimes he now knows what century and sometimes what year we're in, but not the season, month, or day. He can't bring up the names of either son-in-law or of the president he so despises. He can't get his bearings outdoors, recognize the turn to our building, understand the bus or subway routes. He panics as we cross the street, certain that oncoming cars will run us over, yet he lacks the patience and knowledge to wait for the light to change—such inference is beyond him. He's especially frightened of turning cars, unable to trust their drivers not to cut us down before we get across. He can't order food from a menu or calculate a tip. He frequently forgets to flush the toilet, selects a weather-inappropriate jacket, deposits his dirty clothes in the newspaper recycle box instead of the laundry basket, and often misses certain spots while shaving. (When I offer to take him to a barber for a shave, he says, "Allow a barber to put a razor to my throat? Never! I have certain standards!") As for the shower, he can't adjust the water temperature, can't remember to use soap, can't open the shampoo, and resists the entire project so strenuously that it's all I can do to get him to submit to one shower a week. Afterward, he thanks me, proclaiming how good he feels, but five minutes later he has forgotten.

Of the Four A's of Dementia Diagnosis listed on the Web,

aphasia, apraxia, amnesia, and *agnosia,* he exhibits all of them in varying degrees. Although he can talk well enough to fool strangers, his aphasia (inability to comprehend language or find the right words to use in communication) shows up when he tries to write himself reminders, which sometimes make little sense ("Do NOT use TV for small news or other meaningful applications!!"). And he remains disablingly afflicted by apraxia (loss of ability to carry out a sequence of activities, like dressing or drawing), amnesia (pathologic impairment of memory), and agnosia (loss of willpower resulting from an inability to carry a thought long enough to determine or pursue a goal). When I ask him the standard diagnostic questions listed on one of the websites, he performs poorly. Out of three points (one per action)—*take this paper in your right hand, fold it in half, and put it on the floor*—he never gets more than two points. If I ask him to do two things at once, for instance, take the napkins and the water to the table, he can manage only one.

He can no longer tell or get a joke, though sometimes if I laugh he'll follow suit. Explanations tire him out. And every day he asks me shocking questions: When will we see your parents (who died ten years ago)? What city are we in? How long have we been together? Are we legally married? Can you please tell me how many children I have?

Most disheartening, he can't acknowledge that there's anything wrong with him, still believes he can do everything, assumes he is the same capable, helpful man I married.

In short, as the second year proceeds, his mind is still severely and probably—as I'm finally beginning to allow—permanently impaired. Somewhere inside me I know that the moment may never arrive, as it did after his yearlong recovery from heart surgery, when we can resume our former lives. Never again will we be able to mull over a problem together, negotiate a decision, chew over the news, arrange to meet on a street corner, discuss the meaning of a remark, consult each other for advice, dispute the wisdom of an action, confide our secret anxieties, appreciate each other's wit, plan a trip, weigh our options, fantasize about the future. There'll be no new sculptures of his on the windowsills, no new leather-bound book of mine on the bookshelf.

It seems to me his impairment is deeply connected to memory loss: How can you think or reason without remembering the facts to reflect upon? How do you know which way to turn when you've forgotten where you're trying to go? With no recall of time passing or of what has transpired, you are bound to be in a state of perpetual confusion or apprehension. And along with confusion, agitation and upset. No matter how eagerly you may wish to cooperate, you can't respond to others' expectations if you can't remember what they are. If a minute is the same as an hour, when your wife goes to the bathroom, how do you know she hasn't "evaporated"—and, without her, how you will survive?

And I, presumably in full command of my faculties, with no excuse for forgetting how much he has forgotten, but not yet able to abandon hope, become his nemesis—trying to reason with him when he becomes upset, becoming upset in return as I repeat my mantras with mounting distress:

But I told you I was just going to the bathroom, I said I'd be back in a minute.

Why are you changing your clothes again?

But you promised not to come into the kitchen while I'm cooking.

My god! You've swallowed my pills instead of yours!

Won't you please stay there and watch the game?

No, no—you cannot go out by yourself!

The one time he got away from me was disastrous. We were at the crowded farmer's market in Union Square, stocking up on vegetables. I turned my back on him for a moment to select some corn, and when I turned around again, both he and our shopping cart were gone. As fast as a fly is snatched by a lizard, he disappeared into the Saturday crowd. One moment there, the next moment . . . gone!

I searched the entire market—not a trace. Thinking he might have set off for home, I began traversing the streets between Union Square and our building, fear mounting toward terror with every block. When I returned to our loft to find it empty, panic overtook me, and I called 911. The police picked me up in a squad car, and for two and a half harrowing hours we circled the neighborhood and combed the park before finally receiving a message from the station house that Scott was in the emergency room of the local hospital. We sped there, siren screaming, to find him in a corridor on a gurney, bruised, bloody, and highly agitated, shouting in pain over three grotesquely dislocated fingers on his lacerated right hand. The ambulance driver told us that he'd been found lying on the cobblestones beneath the West Side Highway, far from Union Square, with an empty shopping cart beside him.

Ever since that day, each of us for a different reason panics when the other is out of sight.

In fact, uncannily, we are becoming mirror images of each other. Having left the doctors behind, we have forged a closer, though rawer, marriage. As he loses his self-control I find it increasingly hard to hold on to mine, until it seems as if his illness has infected me. We have become each other's keepers. And goaders. Each day it's something else.

This morning he can't find his wallet anywhere. Sometimes it's his glasses or his watch that's missing, occasionally it's his keys—all bad enough. But losing his wallet is the worst. It contains his Medicare card with his Social Security number printed on it, emergency names and telephone numbers, list of medications, credit card, cash—without which he dare not leave the building. It's probably only misplaced, like all the other missing things that turn up eventually—hidden somewhere and forgotten. But the slim chance that it's actually outside in the world of identity thieves makes it imperative that I cancel our credit cards immediately and begin the time-consuming process of replacing everything. We search inside every drawer, in every pants and jacket pocket, at the back of each shelf, on the floor, under the bed. He gives up quickly, muttering, slamming a cabinet door, but I continue to search, going over the same territory again and again, my own frustration mounting at every swipe until I can hardly suppress my irritation as I caution him: "You simply must stop hiding your wallet. Why do you keep doing it?" (As if the answer——to protect it—were not obvious.) He storms away from me, shouting, "All you ever do is criticize me! I'd be better off dead!"

Though extreme, this turning his feelings against himself rather than against me has deep roots. Years back, when I used to reproach him for failing to listen to what I was saying—when in fact he was simply exhibiting early signs of memory loss—rather than fight back he acceded and withdrew. High-minded and self-controlled, throughout our years together he refused to participate in the petty squabbles I occasionally provoked. Now, however, sometimes our bickering and shouting sound like the hostilities of an ordinary embattled marriage. With this difference: in such a marriage there's always an out—to separate. In our marriage, if we should go our separate ways, his way would be directly to a nursing home.

This man, with whom I go back half a century, whose life has been entwined with mine for decades, and with whom I have lived my most fulfilling years, is too dear to me, too close for me to be able to contemplate that now. For some it might not be bad, possibly even an improvement, but for him, a man who has always been restless and now insists on going outdoors half a dozen times a day, confinement inside would be sheer torment. Easier to imagine his death than putting him away. Yet I'm starting to realize that my faith in his eventual recovery looks increasingly naïve. Facing squarely for the first time the bleak prospect of spending the rest of my days as caretaker of a well-meaning, loving, but helpless and clueless man, I find myself succumbing in odd moments to unexpected bouts of grief, as if a life has ended. Not his life, but mine.

Just as I'm teetering on the verge of despair, a friend gives me *The 36-Hour Day*, the survival manual for caregivers to people with damaged brains. Its main message is: *It's up to you to prevent a crisis before it starts by remaining calm, gentle, and understanding.* Since "people with brain diseases often become excessively upset," and "most of these behaviors are not under his control," "the best way to manage catastrophic reactions is to stop them before they happen."

Like reading Dr. Spock when my children were little, reading *The 36-Hour Day*, with its useful tips on how to cope and its descriptions that render the strange familiar, is reassuring. Throughout its pages Scott's disturbing behaviors—always following behind me like a puppy ("shadowing"), putting his clothes on backward, hiding things, cursing and insulting caregivers—are revealed as typical of his condition, as my responses are all too typical of mine. That book has nailed us, filling me with waves of guilt but also with a certain relief, even comfort.

The book shows me how deluded I've been to assume that the odd, frightening, annoying, or dangerous behaviors that overtook Scott after he fell would gradually disappear as he recovered, returning us to normal life. In fact, the opposite happens. The stronger he gets, the more unfathomable—and unacceptable—he finds his limitations: Now that he can walk normally, he thinks he should be free to go out whenever he likes. Physically able to dress himself again, he sees nothing wrong with leaving his pajamas on under his street clothes or never changing his socks. Eager to pull his weight in the kitchen as he once did, he puts dirty dishes away in the cupboards and mixes up the flatware in the drawers. Everything is a struggle. He resents my prohibitions and urgings; my explanations enrage him. "Baloncy!" he shouts (still the gentleman). Whereas during the first year he spent his time lying on the couch by himself, content to look out the window for hours on end, now that his energy has increased, he demands my constant and unwavering attention. Worse, he is often raring to go out but with no notion of where. Some days are sweet—whenever I'm willing to devote myself to him exclusively (and after all, how oppressive can it be to sip cappuccino at a favorite café or watch a movie?)—but other days are peppered with bickering and strife, accusations and resentment. Which, if the authors of the book are correct, will only worsen unless I resign myself truly and completely to his condition, which he cannot help.

How ironic that when he was furthest from himself, hope sustained me, enabling me to help him back, but now that he's better, hope undermines me. Yet without that lifeline, how will I survive? I fear that to resign myself to the status quo and abandon hope is not only to betray myself but to abandon him—as Medicare dumps patients who are no longer improving, leaving on their own the millions of elderly in desperate need of humane long-term care, before returning to pick up their hospice costs as death approaches.

Rather than accept his limitations, sometimes it seems to me kinder to fight him—as if I could force him to remember by sheer repetition or by shouting my say or by leaving a trail of notes in black Magic Marker (REMEMBER TO FLUSH THE TOILET! PLEASE TURN THE CLOSET LIGHT <u>OFF</u>), which, though he reads them faithfully, fail to penetrate enough for him to act upon. But such pigheaded determination ignores the message of the book. If I am to avoid despair, in this second year I must resign myself to his condition by trading my first-year faith in his recovery for full acceptance of his permanent impairment. If despair is the opposite of hope, then acceptance must lie somewhere in between. Neither despair nor hope, cautions the book. Only accept.

SIX

Could Happen

The loft next door to ours comes on the market. For years we'd been eyeing it as a studio for Scott but could never afford it. Though smaller than our loft, it has the same high ceilings, shapely columns, and tall windows ours has. Having moved the contents of his studio to mini-storage when the lease was up six months ago, I suddenly see the loft next door as the solution to our problems. If it were ours, I could hire a caregiver who, in exchange for the privilege of living in that lovely space, could entertain him there for a certain number of hours each day and help him make art while I stay home and write again. With only a wall between us, we'd be both near and far enough from each other to work without anxiety and then could spend the rest of our time together.

In the absence of a health-care system providing long-term care for any citizen who requires it, as any decent system must do, Scott's daughter, who became a successful venture capitalist in the wild 1990s, steps up and offers to buy the loft for her father's benefit. With Manhattan real estate always a promising investment, she agrees to hold on to it until he "no longer needs it" (read: death or nursing home). Fortuitously, the monthly maintenance, which we will pay, is exactly the same as the rent on his former studio.

Nothing like action to raise the spirits! Once the negotiations have been completed, I launch an all-out search for a suitable companion for Scott, posting an ad to "Exchange Chelsea Loft for Part-Time Companion to Brain-Injured Artist" on both the employment and housing websites of nearby colleges. With good housing in shorter supply than part-time jobs, our offer is a dream of a deal for the right person—far better than the shared dorm room in exchange for twenty-five hours a week of clerical work that NYU offers its own work/study students.

Three days later the phone begins to ring and afterward seldom stops. Some of the students who apply are only after the housing, but a few—those who are artists themselves or who have grandparents with dementia—seem also drawn by the job.

After many interviews I settle on Karin O'Brien, a twenty-eight-year-old Texas artist, now an NYU graduate student in art, who elected to work her way through college by caring for the elderly. Her father is a neurologist and her mother an internist. I can hardly believe our luck! Besides coveting the new apartment for herself, she seems genuinely interested in Scott, and he in turn is charmed by her. We agree that starting a month from now, in October, when she moves in, every weekday from nine to two she will keep Scott next door or take him out to museums, to galleries, on errands—anywhere, I don't care, as long as he's not with me. The rest of the time I'll be his caregiver, and the new loft will be hers, though we agree to call it "Scott's studio."

Before I move the contents of his former studio in from storage and before Karin moves in, hoping to inspire him to resume his art, I decide to use the empty space to mount a whirlwind show of his "recent works on paper"—works I've somehow managed to cajole or drag out of him stroke by stroke and piece by piece in daily ten-minute sessions in our living room, despite his invariable grumbling resistance. I've learned how difficult it is for someone with a frontal-lobe brain injury to be able to form and carry out a plan, as artists, particularly sculptors, must. The art therapist I briefly hired had even less success than I in getting him to work, now that Memory, mother of the Muses, has deserted him.

Still, my dream is that once his old studio is reconstructed in the new space, he will be inspired to work again. It's well-known that de Kooning's Alzheimer's did nothing to slow him down; once Scott is surrounded again by his work, perhaps Karin, an artist herself, will be able to reawaken his twenty-year passion for art making. I'm counting on it; she must—because, incapable of sustained reading, too disoriented to go safely outside on his own, unable to conceive much less pursue a project, if he doesn't start doing art again, I'm afraid he will have nothing to do for the rest of his life but dog my footsteps or gaze out the window.

A year after we moved in together, Scott announced that he was taking early retirement. I was terrified that despite his promise, he would hang around home while I was trying to work, but I needn't have worried. He immediately set off to fulfill his boyhood dream of being an artist, a dream born at the National Gallery of Art in Washington, D.C., where his uncle, who was chief superintendent of the museum's physical plant, allowed the smitten boy to wander freely through the galleries whenever his parents brought him south to visit.

After choosing marble as his medium, he joined a studio run by a well-known sculptor, who became Scott's teacher and mentor. For two years he studied diligently, working days, nights, and weekends, bringing home one large marble sculpture after another until he felt he had produced enough work to present to galleries. He applied to the cooperative Pleiades Gallery in Soho, which soon enough agreed to mount a solo show for him. He worked tirelessly on that show, selecting the pieces, having them photographed, assembling bases for them, compiling publicity lists. That accomplished, he began entering his work in competitions for group shows, with increasing success. He even found a gallery in Honolulu when we settled there in 1991, only three years after he had first taken up hammer and chisel. In the university art department's foundry, he learned to make molds of his pieces and cast them himself—until he collapsed with the aneurysm and abandoned casting for good.

When his doctors warned that working again in stone would strain his heart, he began experimenting with other, lighter materials: papier-mâché, Styrofoam, wax, clay, plastic, mixed media. Deciding against spending any more creative energy on the time-consuming business of exhibiting his work, he produced hundreds of drawings and paintings of every size, including a round masterpiece, six feet in diameter, of subtle blues and roses and touches of gold that changes dramatically, depending on the light and time of day, like the very cosmos it evokes. We rolled it home from his studio along the sidewalk and hung it on the wall facing our bed, where it greets us each morning like a second dawn.

After that, he began a series of small clay and wax pieces that he had cast in bronze, coveted by everyone who saw them. I hated to part with a single one, but believing he could always make more, reluctantly I did. Soon, despite the doctors' warnings, he returned to stone, his first love, starting off with smaller pieces than before but gradually edging up toward larger ones. Again, he worked diligently and joyfully every day, ignoring the

risks. If his work shortened his life, he said, it would probably
be worth it.

In the end, it wasn't his sculpture that did him in. It was the
studio he built for me in Maine without installing a proper
guardrail in the sleeping loft. Or the dawning dementia, probably a result of those seven hours on the heart-lung machine
while the doctors repaired his aorta, which saved his life but
may have left him confused as to which way to turn in the
dark. Or perhaps, as he would maintain, it was simply the diminished awareness and reaction time that accompany old age.

Some of Scott's post-fall art is continuous with his previous
work, but some of it is unlike anything he ever did before—
especially the group of drawings consisting of one or two words
fancifully drawn in many colors and designs:

> *Why?*
> *Why not?*
> *Yes*
> *No*
> *Yes No*
> *Maybe*
> *No!*
> *Yes Yes Yes*
> *OK*
> *OK Maybe*
> *Could Happen*

Are these the questions he ponders while he lies on the
couch looking off into space? Are these the concepts his injured brain must grapple with? I can think of no drawing or

painting from before his fall that depicted words, let alone such primal words as these. His new drawings have stripped reflection down to its essentials: why, why not, yes, no, maybe—so much simpler than the first post-fall writing he produced for the speech therapist at Rusk:

> The Earth is the central organizer for thoughts, concepts, and progressive deeds. Our births are real but our deeds are very random.

The therapist saw in these sentences only the disorganized ramblings of a mind afflicted with fluent aphasia, but to me they seemed reassuring, revealing that he was still capable of deep reflection. To atheists like us, the earth, that is, the intractable world of matter, is indeed the basis or "central organizer" of consciousness—meaning "thoughts and concepts." Our births are real, but after that, all bets are off. Once you are in this world, randomness rules—look at what happened to him! Just so, the new drawings—*Yes, No, Why, Could Happen*—seem to summarize the lessons of his accident: anything can happen at any time; nothing is ever guaranteed.

The poem "Could Have," by the Polish Nobel laureate Wisława Szymborska, perfectly captures the mysterious, incomprehensible contingency of life that now and forevermore will haunt us:

> It could have happened.
> It had to happen.
> It happened earlier. Later.
> Nearer. Farther off.
> It happened, but not to you.
>
> You were saved because you were the first.
> You were saved because you were the last.

Alone. With others.
On the right. The left.
Because it was raining. Because of the shade.
Because the day was sunny.

You were in luck—there was a forest.
You were in luck—there were no trees.
You were in luck—a rake, a hook, a beam, a brake,
a jamb, a turn, a quarter inch, an instant.
You were in luck—just then a straw went floating by.

As a result, because, although, despite.
What would have happened if a hand, a foot
Within an inch, a hairsbreadth from
An unfortunate coincidence

So you're here? Still dizzy from another dodge, close shave,
    reprieve?
One hole in the net and you slipped through?
I couldn't be more shocked or speechless.
Listen,
How your heart pounds inside me.

For weeks I devote myself to preparing for the show. It will
be Scott's reentry into the world, a year and two months after
the accident. Our closest friends come through for us: Susan
and Carol, both artists, cull five groups of drawings from Scott's
surprisingly large recent production and figure out how to
hang them. Polly's husband, Andrew, a graphic designer, designs
the invitation, using the drawing *Could Happen* as the show's
title image. Linda helps order the champagne and food. Ann
supplies the guest book. I clean and clean and clean. In hom-
age to Scott's earlier art, I set up a long table on two sawhorses
to hold a dozen of his small bronze sculptures, plus a few of

stone, from the years preceding the accident, which we move next door piece by piece. Then we carry in tables for food, a few folding chairs, champagne flutes, plates, napkins, an ice bucket.

Since it's impossible for me to accomplish much with him trailing behind me, agitated, demanding, and confused, I call an agency to send an aide to stay with him in our loft during the final days before the show so we can hang the pictures and finish the preparations efficiently. But he'll have none of her. When she tells him not to go next door, he curses her out and yells at her, stranger and jailer, until I have no choice but to dismiss her. I hire another aide, but it's the same story. So he accompanies me back and forth between the two lofts.

At last the day of the opening arrives: Sunday, September 25, 2005. It's a brilliant afternoon, unseasonably warm; the sun beams in through the tall windows to light up Scott's startling art. Guests begin to drift in, many bearing flowers, until the edges of the tables and the windowsills are filled with bouquets of roses, carnations, freesias, tulips. There are perhaps sixty people, most of whom haven't seen Scott since his fall. He greets them warmly, pretending to recognize each one. Hello! Hello! Hello! When they express delight at how surprisingly well he looks, he has no idea what they're talking about, but he's able to compensate sufficiently that they never guess it. He manages to hold up his side of each brief conversation, answering questions as if his responses bear some relation to the truth, and no one is the wiser. Karin, who has come to help me manage the party, twice takes Scott back to our loft for a brief rest; each time, he returns refreshed, ready for more. True to character, he rejects our friends' praises with self-deprecating modesty, but I know he is gratified by both the praise and the show itself. By the time the party's over and the guests have gone home, confirmed in their expectation of the full recovery intimated by my misleadingly optimistic e-mails, Scott, whose long-term memory knows what effort goes into mounting a show, begins to praise and thank me for "doing all this work— for me." That night and all the next day, while the pictures are still up, he keeps on thanking me, kissing my hands and saying over and over how happy he is. It is all I hoped for.

But once the show has been taken down, he has no memory of it, not even that it occurred. None. And again I face the recurring question: Was it—is it—worth the effort? If so, for whom? I had thought it was for him, but if he remembers nothing? Then was it for the guests, who have been misleadingly reassured? For me?

The day after the art comes down, a truckload of his things arrives from mini-storage. Tools, equipment; portfolios of drawings, scores of paintings, stones large and small; plus shelving, tables, chairs, lamps, books, all stacked in jumbled piles against the walls. The following day the movers return to help me create order. Since the new space is larger than the old studio, we set up separate areas for work and living.

Our new lives are ready to begin.

Karin moves into the studio, giving me five precious hours of freedom each weekday. Exactly as I did when my children started preschool, leaving me alone for three hours a day, as soon as Karin picks up Scott, I turn off the telephone and go to work, writing about my life with him.

I hadn't expected to write about so private and raw a subject until a friend in whom I'd been confiding, who happens to be an editor, kept insisting that a truthful account of the turn our lives have taken could make a worthy book. At first I was skeptical, but since we were winging everything else in our new, uncharted lives, I gradually warmed to the idea. Certainly no other subject was closer to my thoughts, and there was the possibility that writing about it could help me understand it. Why not try? Scott was all for it. I decided to read him the chapters as I wrote them and allow him the final say (though in the end, supportive as ever, he didn't object to a single word).

So it happens that at nine o'clock each morning I banish the real Scott in order to entertain the virtual one, who stays with me on the page until two, when the real one opens our door, exclaiming, "Look who it is! It's my beautiful wife!" and hugs me like a returning warrior.

Meanwhile, in the other loft, Karin tries every trick she knows to get Scott to sculpt or draw again, but he strenuously resists, except occasionally when she cajoles him into working alongside her on a joint drawing. It saddens me to see that he can no longer do what once most enthralled him. Is it because he somehow knows his new work won't measure up to the old, or is it simply a consequence of the damage to his frontal cortex? To make the simplest drawing requires deciding what to draw, what medium to use, what scale, what colors, where to put the first mark, then the next—all still beyond him.

I make my pact with the devil—or is it with an angel? I'm not sure. As long as I have five uninterrupted hours to myself, I'll give the rest of my time ungrudgingly to him. I know the deal will work only if I attempt nothing for myself during my hours with him—no work, no reading, no telephoning. Hardly my preferred way of life, but if I fail, we'll be plagued by discord and resentment, a devil's punishment, and if I succeed, I will be rewarded with an angel's gift of tranquillity. I've seen the writing in *The 36-Hour Day*: resign myself truly and completely to his condition or be doomed to a life of conflict.

Weekends of unrelenting caregiving are hard, but by the time Karin goes home to Texas for Christmas break, I've just about mastered the art. Knowing she'll soon be back, I put away my manuscript and with it my desires. Like tourists, we take in the pleasures of the city, as we did back on those Tuesday afternoons when we first moved in together, and though we now move slowly, cautiously along the holiday-crowded streets like ordinary people growing old, we usher in 2006 at two New Year's parties as if nothing had changed. Bathed in my attention, Scott is as happy and adoring as a child.

I e-mail Linda: "Since Karin left for vacation, we've been having many consecutive conflict-free love-filled tranquil days. I think I now know the secret: don't desire to do anything for myself. Spend all our time together—his deepest desire. No will, no longing; no resentment, no conflict. Simple and rewarding."

To which she responds, "Are the love-filled days the greater good for you (for *you*)? Isn't there anything you'd prefer to do in those hours you spend together?"

Of course I'd prefer to have our old life back, to be on my own to write and think while Scott goes off to his studio. But that's not an option. And if I try doing work while he's around, our days are ruined. Why choose unhappiness? Far better to have second-best days than ones spoiled by conflict or poisoned by resentment. Like youth—foolish to want it back, especially when age has its own rewards.

I'd like to ask you a question when you have a moment," says Scott, coming over to my desk, where I'm answering e-mail. I complete the message, then: "What is it?" though I know what he's going to ask. He has only three questions left in his repertoire: *What can I do to help you? When are we going to see the children?* and the third one, which he asks half a dozen times a day and is now on the verge of popping—

"May I take you out to eat?" Even if we've just finished eating and are hours away from the next mealtime, this is the question of any hour.

"No, we're eating home tonight. I've already started dinner."

"Then may I take you out to lunch?"

I shake my head. "We had lunch hours ago. But thanks for asking."

Beginning on the day he reappeared in my life and refused to touch those hors d'oeuvres I'd prepared for him, this clash became one of our most frequent struggles: my wanting to cook versus his wanting to go out. He simply would not believe that cooking is a creative joy for me. Instead, he viewed it as some sort of gender-based sacrifice that exposed him as a sexist exploiter—a self-image so unacceptable that he would do almost anything to avoid it. (Anything, that is, except cook for us. In fact, during the summers while I was in Maine he often bought vegetables at the farmer's market in Union Square and took them home to steam and eat over couscous or pasta. But he insisted such fare was too "simple" to serve to me and instead attempted recipes so complicated and difficult that, though worthy of me in his estimation, were guaranteed to fail, and he soon gave up in defeat.)

His guilty pleasure at my table, intensified by his keen appreciation of my cooking, may have been sparked by an article I'd once written called "A Marriage Agreement," which proposed that a couple ought to split all their household chores equally. Or perhaps it began with his first wife's aversion to cooking. Whatever the cause, to spare me the work and himself the guilt, he adopted the only solution he could think of: restaurants.

When, after years of trying, I finally convinced him that I genuinely love to cook, preferring quiet evenings at home to running around, he agreed to limit his dinner invitations to once or twice a week, and to stay out of the kitchen while I prepared our meals, providing he could do the cleanup. That arrangement, a triumph of compromise and culinary pleasure—which for one season he recorded by photographing every dinner—held until the day he fell. And now here we are again, waging the old battle.

"May I take you out to lunch?" he repeats, in the grip of his fixation.

Tired of explaining, and knowing he won't remember anyway, I offer, "Not today, but maybe tomorrow if you like," adopting the *creative lying* recommended by an advice sheet for caregivers. Or I resort to the all-purpose hedge universally used on children: "We'll see."

❦

Just as I've begun to accept the full implications of Scott's condition, now that the healing year has passed, he takes another turn for the better in the crucial cognitive and memory departments, and the terrifying roller-coaster ride I had thought was over starts back up. Dare I hope again?

One minute he's lying in front of the windows as usual, looking up at the red Japanese paper lanterns hanging from the ceiling, and the next minute he's pushing himself up to standing, rolling up a newspaper, and waving it at the lanterns to stir enough air to move them.

I stand transfixed, hardly able to believe what I'm seeing. A display of initiative as I haven't seen since before his accident! He has a desire, transforms it into a rational plan, remembers the plan, summons the energy, and executes it, waving the newspaper harder and harder until he almost succeeds in his goal. But he's not quite strong enough, and soon he returns to lying on the couch.

"What were you doing just now?"

"I was trying to get one of those lanterns to move, but I'm afraid it didn't work."

"But it will when you're stronger. Here—I'll open a window and let the winter breeze do it."

Then I run to my computer to e-mail a report of this momentous event to my closest friends and family.

Karin reports that her pressure too occasionally pays off: if she chooses the medium and the subject and gets him started, he's ready to draw a little. Every couple of weeks she brings over a drawing he's made—now one of elephants, now one of a sailboat against the city skyline, and now a vibrant, vivacious picture of purple flowers, a harbinger of spring.

His memory is unquestionably improving. When the phlebotomist, who has reduced her visits from daily to monthly now that his clotting time has stabilized, calls to make an appointment to draw his blood the following morning, I inform Scott as a courtesy, hardly expecting him to remember. In bed the next morning, as soon as he opens his eyes, he astonishes me by asking, "What time is the vampire coming to suck my blood?" All across the rugged mountain of night and the hazardous path of sleep he has remembered this fact—not an old memory, but a new one. I rejoice as if he were my child taking his very first step.

And more! At dinner one night, watching me listening to music on the radio in a semi-trance, he asks, "What are you thinking?" and when I shake my head, he adds, "A penny for your thoughts." That he wants to know what I'm thinking reveals a new awareness, long lost to him, that each mind is a separate inner world that no other person can enter without an invitation, a world of secrets. If my thoughts are worth a penny to him, his newly recovered knowledge is worth a million to me.

One Saturday morning he is suddenly eager for us to get out the door and going. (His greatest compliment to me these days, uttered with breathless admiration, is "You're such a good goer.") "What's the hurry?" I ask. "It's still early." To which he replies, "The day's going by. Staying inside is a big waste of time."

How much healing is revealed by that giddy phrase, a *waste of time*! First there's the concept of *time* itself, no mean recovery. Now when I ask him what year it is, he usually answers correctly, instead of saying 2004 (the year of his fall), as he said through the entire year following. And contained within the concept of time as something limited, useful, not to be wasted is the idea of the *future*, with its close relation to *effort* and *accomplishment*. Can these powerful engines be coming back?

Finally, the moment arrives when he is able to brave the many confusing, ad-cluttered pages of *Time* magazine to locate for me near the back a small review of Polly's first book. Instead of abandoning this challenging quest after a few pages, he manages to keep the goal in mind through the entire search until he can proclaim, "Here it is!" and "Wait till you read this!"

As he is better, I am better—thrilled and energized. But as he is also worse, I am worse. Again—the better, the worse.

Nothing I've read has led me to expect that each of his improvements will be accompanied by an expansion of his desires and, in turn, of their frustration, rendering this once supremely courteous, self-controlled man an increasingly volatile stranger. Seeing his progress, I allow myself to expect more of him than he can manage, and my frustration swells along with his. When he calls for the check before the main course has arrived, when he insists on leaving the theater for the bathroom precisely at the movie's climax, when he tears a big chunk out of the cake I've just baked for a party, my surprise and irritation erupt before I can suppress them, to which he responds with explosive, sometimes frightening outbursts. The most frequent are over his desire to go out alone.

Why shouldn't I? I've gone out alone all my life.

Because it's not safe anymore.

That's ridiculous. What could happen?

You could get lost. Or hurt.

Then I'm a prisoner in my own home!

Not a prisoner. Someone with a brain injury.

You're bringing that up again? I don't want to hear it!

And within moments he's storming off again toward the door, and again I must either jolly or threaten him out of leaving. Sometimes I think, Okay then, go! Get lost! Destroy yourself! But the thought remains unspoken, and I have no choice but to drop what I'm doing, shove my feet into a pair of shoes, grab a coat, and, even if I'm seething with resentment, dash after him out the door.

Yet goodwill invariably rescues us. As soon as the provocation is over, our anger disappears: his because he can't remember the problem, mine because I can't forget the cause.

Occasionally he's the one to restore the peace. In the midst of one fight, despite his cognitive disadvantage, he brings a framed photo of me from his dresser to the kitchen, sets it down before me, and says, "Take a good look. This is the wife I used to have," melting my anger into stinging remorse. We have always been quick to make up and forgive, but now forgiveness is superfluous. Since he has no control over any of his reactions, then no matter who may have started it, I'm the one obliged to end it—by distracting him with a task (so eager is he to be helpful) or with a kiss, that fairy-tale trick for changing the beast back into a prince. The admonition in *The 36-Hour Day* (reduced by Karin to thirty-one hours except on weekends), that *it's up to you to prevent a crisis before it starts by remain-*

ing calm, gentle, and understanding, still holds, however much he has improved.

If this is my burden, there's also a secret reprieve: every impulsive, angry, cruel, or foolish thing I say or do, he'll immediately, mercifully forget.

Even after I accept Scott's impairment as permanent and acknowledge that the painstaking attentiveness required for making art will probably never return, I sometimes catch myself expecting that one day, if I'm only patient and good, our lives will go back to normal. This irrational hope keeps me trying to teach him old tricks and show him how to improve. On the inside of our door, with its three locks, I have placed three notes: two say "DON'T TURN THIS LOCK" and one says "USE THIS LOCK ONLY!" The notes have been up for a year and a half, to little avail: most of the time he still can't get it right. Nevertheless, I can't bring myself to give up and remove them. I forget that our lives are already normal, our new normal, that this is what our life is now, with its daily pleasures and obstacles, as our former lives were normal then.

If I'm honest, I see that other phases of my life have been worse—like the low point of divorcing, with its inevitable toll on our children. So potent was my anxiety during that stressful time that sometimes I feared that even after everything was settled, things might continue to worsen and maybe never get better.

And now look. After that divorce, two decades of love.

❧

It's one of those vibrant Sunday afternoons in early April that is the glory of a Manhattan spring. The cafés are filling up with young people rushing the season in sandals and short-sleeved

T-shirts, soaking up the sun. Who would not be elated to walk down Seventh Avenue—or for that matter any major avenue of the West Village, from Fifth to Eighth, or Bleecker to Hudson—and suddenly turn one's gaze onto the streets to the east or to the west to be stunned anew by the sudden explosion of flowering trees forming a canopy of white or pink blossoms in front of the old town houses. "Isn't that just glorious!" exclaims Scott with an astonished inward rush of breath. On the hard city pavements the mere sight of those trees shimmering in the sunlight must raise even the most distressed spirits, no matter how many Manhattan springs (for me, more than fifty) one has experienced or (for him) forgotten. In the side streets there are dozens of tiny, enchanting front gardens already filled to their borders with brilliantly colored tulips and daffodils and pansies, and window boxes overflowing with geraniums.

How will we ever choose among the restaurants with their irresistible aroma of freshly brewed coffee, or the sidewalk cafés overflowing with lively people sipping mimosas or Bloody Marys as they dig into their eggs Benedict or mushroom-and-spinach omelets garnished with field greens and home fries?

"You choose," says Scott. "I don't care, as long as we're together."

Though he is able to rejoice in the spring awakening and relish a weekend brunch, three months shy of two years since the accident he still can't make the simplest decision. And the experts, no matter how much they know about the brain, still have no help to offer.

It has long been known that particular locations in the brain control certain complex tasks, because damage to those areas, whether through injury or disease, causes loss of specific functions—like the ability to understand and express language, recognize faces and other sorts of objects, see colors, process sounds, move parts of your body. The Internet is full of diagrams of that majestic organ, showing its two hemispheres and the various parts and their functions. In general, language, mathematics, and abstract reasoning are centered in the left hemisphere, while visual and spatial information and functions like dancing and athletics are centered in the right. Very roughly, the frontal lobes control the "higher functions" of cognition, concentration, planning, and emotional control; the temporal lobes deal with hearing and language; the parietal lobes with body orientation; the occipital lobes with visual interpretation; the limbic lobes with sex and emotions. In these ways and more, human brains are all alike. But this knowledge has so far done little to enable healing. Other than keeping the patient stimulated and engaged, there are few effective treatments for TBI except the passage of time—and how much time, no one can predict. Clips I've saved from *The New York Times* report one brain trauma victim recovering speech after nineteen years of muteness and another returning to family life after ten years without affect or memory, even though, as one professor of rehab medicine is quoted as saying, "Once brain-injured you are always brain-injured, for the rest of your life . . . There is no cure, there is only intensive compensation." Physical therapy may train someone to walk again or improve dexterity and coordination; cognitive remediation therapy may increase one's attention and concentration through simple repetitive mental exercises ("That's not for me," cautions Scott sternly as I read him this paragraph. "I just want to be myself"); and in place of impaired memory, for which there is no cure, patients are encouraged to develop such compensatory strategies as writing copious notes to themselves (which they must somehow remember to consult), or else, like Scott, rely on someone else to do their remembering for them.

As for the degenerative dementias associated with old age, in which cells die, neural connections wither, and the brain

gradually shrivels up—such as Alzheimer's, with its characteristic plaques and tangles obstructing the brain's neurons and de-
tectable only during autopsy; vascular dementia, resulting from
a series of tiny strokes; or age-related memory impairment
(ARMI)—they are currently one-way tickets to oblivion. So
little is known about their cause and cure that at least one prom-
inent neurologist (Peter Whitehouse, in *The Myth of Alzheimer's*)
believes that between normal aging and Alzheimer's there is no
clear line, and that the few pills that are claimed to slow down
decline (admittedly, by no more than six months, a pittance)
may benefit the pharmaceutical companies more than the patients.

In Scott's case, both TBI and the irreversible dementia that
probably started with his heart surgery and accelerated explo-
sively with his fall are in play, and how these two trajectories
will impact each other remains so mysterious and unpredictable
that not one doctor will hazard a guess. Once again, irony
rules. If time is the one thing working in Scott's favor when it
comes to TBI, it's also working against him when it comes to
the dementia. The former, time alone may help, while the lat-
ter, time can only worsen. Entering the final stretch, better and
worse again run neck and neck, racing each other against time.

❧

The day after our Sunday outing, I call our accountant for an
appointment to go over our income tax data, offering him the
choice of a morning date with me alone or an afternoon date
with me and Scott.

"Afternoon, of course," he says.

I'm surprised. During this, his most harried time of year, I
would have expected him to opt for the briefest possible meeting, hardly likely if Scott's along. "Really? Why?"

"Because Scott is one of my very favorite individuals in the entire world. He is an absolutely perfect gentleman. I respect and admire him beyond words." Then he adds, as if in warning, "I don't care what you tell me happened to him, he conducts himself like nobody I ever met, and he will never be less than that to me."

I never guessed that Scott had made such a strong impression—especially on someone he saw only once a year at tax time. The effect of his arresting good looks and his sweetness, which impress even strangers, I couldn't fail to observe. (At the party I gave at our loft to introduce him to my friends when he first moved to New York, Hope whispered in my ear, "He's *divine!*" And another friend who was there that day recently confessed how much she envied me when she first met him, leaving unsaid the implication that she no longer does.) But others' opinions of him continue to surprise me.

His dentist, for instance, expresses his affection for Scott to the Scott Watcher to whom I recommended him, which she reports to me by e-mail:

> The doctor told me how he always tries to schedule a full hour with Scott, so they can talk for the first 30 minutes, and then he can look at his teeth after, because even if he's had a bad day Scott always makes him smile—how he comes in, jokes about it, always so positive, an unusual and special quality. And how they get along so well because Scott's father and uncle (right?) were dentists. And he said how fond of him he has grown in the past 7 years. Of course [she added], I wasn't surprised!

At dinner with Susan and Carol, with whom I've been friends since long before Scott reentered my life, Susan begins to speak with barely controlled emotion about Scott's absence from the table. "You are one of my oldest friends, and I love you, but I miss Scott more than I think you know."

"Really! What is it you miss?"

"For one thing, he was always the smartest person in the room. He was the one I counted on to tell me the hard facts, what was what—about politics, economics, the way the world works. He explained things to me I didn't understand, and if I was unsure, I'd adopt his point of view. And he was always so generous and helpful. I miss all of that."

"Yes," says Carol, "I do too. Not to minimize the intellect and insight, but what I miss is the comfort he gave. He was so sweet, so charming, so appreciative." Then, shaking her head slowly: "Such a loss on so many levels."

Again: surprise. Where have I been that I didn't know what he meant to them, but only what he means to me?

Now that my curiosity is aroused, I ask Polly what she particularly misses in him, and she e-mails back:

> He used to notice everything. He was so aware of how things were constructed, where things were, what they were made of—a deep, intellectual curiosity about the physical world. And his sweet, modest way of explaining things, always informative and never pompous or full of himself. And his impatience, too; that's still around, of course. And the way he was so devoted to you; that's still around, too.

I recall his daughter suddenly weeping into the phone over her loss of Scott's frequent advice and counsel, as she telephones to discuss a business problem instead with (paltry substitute) me.

To each one he represented something else: perfect gentle-man, cheerful joker, man of the world, comforter, aware, observing eye, trusted adviser. And though each of these reactions surprises me, he's recognizable in all of them. Couched mainly in the past tense, they sound like tributes at a wake, honoring the man he used to be. This is far kinder than the reaction of many people, who, finding it difficult to look suffering in the eye without feeling fear, horror, and dread, recoil from the demented as if they were contagious or block them out as if they were dead—which may account for the paucity of visitors in nursing homes. But for me, who must daily reconcile the bizarre disjunction of then and now, he makes his impact most vividly in the ever-continuing, surprising present tense.

Just before the deadline, I write out checks for last year's taxes and for this year's estimated taxes, two to the IRS and two to the state. I put them into envelopes, with the appropriate returns and vouchers, and address them carefully. After Scott affixes the stamps and return labels, I place all four envelopes where we always put our outgoing mail, under the cloth on the cabinet in the entrance hallway.

But the next morning, a Saturday, when I look for them to take to the post office, they aren't there.

I begin to search, looking everywhere without success. With a sinking feeling I recall that during all the years we did our taxes together, Scott at one table, I at another, he would be grumpy and cross for days, until the task was done and the returns in the mail. I had thought that since I'd taken over our finances, he would finally be free of tax-time worries. Evidently not.

"Where do you think you could have hidden those envelopes?" I ask him.

"Me! Why would I do a thing like that?" he answers indignantly.

After an hour of steady searching I finally find them in the closet on one of Scott's shelves, hidden among his sweaters. He is shaken. Whereas earlier he was annoyed at my suggestion that he'd had anything to do with their disappearance, now he sits slumped in a chair, repentant, saying over and over, "Oh my god" and "How could I have done such a stupid thing?"

We set off for the post office. By now it is late morning; the line will be long. In fact, it's longer than I've ever seen it— exactly the condition that will bring out his impatience and belligerence. Anticipating that there'll be nowhere for him to sit, as a precaution I've taken along the mail-order folding stool, but for the first time, he refuses to sit on it (another sign of his physical improvement), intent not on comfort, but on *getting the job done*. He can't grasp the fact that there is a single line feeding all five windows and that it won't do to jump the line and go directly to one of them. As I try repeatedly to explain, he clenches his teeth and mutters under his breath, till I sense that it will be only moments before he's shouting "Get your fucking face away from me!"

Finally, in the nick of time, it's our turn at the window, and we leave the post office without calamity. I'm pleased to have managed to keep my cool, but the ordeal has been too much for him. On the way home he stops right in the middle of Seventh Avenue traffic to yell at the driver of a large truck waiting to make a turn. As he whacks the truck repeatedly with his hat and plastic bag, I finally lose it myself, furious that he has so little sense of danger and propriety.

"That truck is a weapon! He could run you down. How dumb is it to attack a truck and scream at the driver in the middle of traffic?" Ignoring how much dumber it is of me to go on hoping that I can change him by invoking reason. I have violated item number one on a one-page list of "Coping and Caring Techniques for Caregivers" I recently downloaded:

Avoid denials and negative answers or orders. Try not to say "no" or "don't." Try not to disagree or argue. Try

not to respond at all if responses will not be positive, or
at least neutral. Answer negative questions indirectly, if
at all.

We're a block away from home, with no more streets to
cross. Knowing he'll follow me, I stomp off down the sidewalk,
turn into our street, and enter our building, letting the door
shut behind me.

Now who's the one ignoring the consequences of irrational
behavior?

Before the elevator arrives, I'm contrite and a little scared,
though not enough to go back outside to get him. Instead, I
hang around the lobby checking our mailbox, keeping an anx-
ious eye on the door.

And there he is, my darling, fumbling with his keys. He
comes into the building greeting neighbors with a smile, completely oblivious of our fight, and I'm off the hook—except
before myself.

The final "technique" on the new list is scant consolation:
*Allow yourself mistakes. Try not to feel guilty over anger. Remember,
you're only human.*

SEVEN

Traveling On

For one entire year following his fall, I gave myself over to healing him. But in the second year, as I became reconciled to his permanent impairment, I had to adjust my goal. Instead of directing every effort toward his recovery, I turned to constructing for us as satisfying a life as possible, which would include time for him and for my own work as well. ("And your goal?" I ask him. "That's easy," he says. "To keep you loving me.")

His work, I finally concede, is finished, in spite of the occasional drawing he does with Karin and his insistence that of course he still does art, just "not today." Cruel to keep urging him to try when he so strenuously resists. Left to himself, he prefers simply to hang around me—perching directly behind me on the love seat while I'm at my computer, propped against pillows on our bed while I dress, seated on the uncomfortable slat-backed chair facing the kitchen as I cook—or else to lie on the couch observing the red lanterns and the blue sky, asking every few minutes, from the depths of his supportive core, "What should I be doing now?" and "How can I help?"— reminders that his condition, rather than liberating him from desire, has left him feeling guilty over "not pulling" his "weight." "You do everything around here and I do nothing," he protests. "How can you stand to put up with me?"

Shall I think up time-consuming tasks to give him, requiring my constant supervision, to make him feel useful, as one might for a child? Unlike a child, he can't learn from them, so what's the point? Instead, I try to comfort him with *from each according to his ability, to each according to his need* or *for better and for worse, in sickness and in health* and plan diversions to amuse us both. Which turn out to be pretty much the very things we always did, only now, instead of doing them on weekends or holidays, they become our daily routines, until our lives appear to resemble nothing so much as a perpetual vacation as we set off each afternoon to follow our fancy wherever it leads, sharing not only meals but afternoon coffee or tea.

Each day, after we get the mail, while I open the bills Scott looks over the steady stream of exotic travel catalogs and says he'd like to "take" me to Africa, to China, to South America, to the Galápagos, to Greece and Turkey—all the places we've never been to together.

I shake my head and laugh. It's hard enough to manage at home, where everything is familiar. He can't begin to imagine the difficulties involved in taking him abroad. Nevertheless, as our lives assume a certain normalcy, the idea of traveling begins to seep back in—first as a renunciation and loss, then as a possibility. As long as we are sentenced to mandatory "vacation," traveling, which I had thought was over, starts to tempt me again, especially since Karin is going home to Texas over spring break, leaving me once more as his sole caregiver. If we could find someplace easy, where the major hurdles would be taken care of, a place we could fly directly to and settle in for a week or so—then why not try? We could certainly use a change of scene.

I consider nearby places, Mexico or a Caribbean island, and think of friends who might be willing to go along with us. Perhaps Polly would come out of kindness. Or else Sarah and George—imagine the swath we'd cut, two lively old women, each trailing a demented spouse.

In the midst of my fantasies, Heather and Norm, in an act of compassion (or pity?) for which I'll be ever grateful, suggest that we join them in Tuscany, where they've rented the "villa" (a recently renovated farmhouse) of a friend for ten days in May, at the end of the NYU term. Norm would do the driving and Heather the navigating, leaving me free to concentrate on Scott. Or, suggests Heather, since the house has a small extra room, I could invite a Scott Watcher to accompany us.

I accept without any hesitation. With Karin unavailable, I ask one of our other Scott Watchers, an NYU senior named Becca, who has never been to Europe and who agrees, in exchange for expenses, never to let Scott out of her sight. I promise myself that if, despite all my precautions, the trip is too hard, we'll turn right around and fly home.

❧

Here we are, darling," I crow. "Finally! Rome."

I look around the Rome airport for the wheelchair I reserved for Scott in hopes that the attendant will whisk us quickly through passport control and customs. I've tried to anticipate every contingency in an effort to make this work. The wheelchair; two rented Italian cell phones, one for Becca and Scott and one for the rest of us, to communicate when we get separated; travel insurance to cover health crises, cancellations, and, for the ultimate contingency, repatriation of remains.

All night long Scott, a lover of maps, has followed our plane's progress on the overhead monitor, yet in the face of my announcement he looks at me uncomprehendingly and says, "This is Rome? You mean the real Rome?"

Heather and Norm grin as I assure Scott, "Yes. The real Rome. Rome, Italy."

He looks around, bewildered. All the signs are in Italian. He's utterly disoriented. "You mean the *real* Rome?" he repeats.

"Yes, the real Rome. But we're not staying here. We're going to drive straight through to Tuscany."

Just outside the double glass doors of international arrivals, where we relinquish the wheelchair, Becca, who preceded us to Italy, greets us. With her olive skin, long black hair, and dark, long-lashed eyes, she could be a native, were it not for the jeans, hooded sweatshirt, sneakers, and backpack that mark her as a traveling American undergrad. From the first moment she hugs Scott and takes his hand, I begin to relax. We ride an elevator and several sets of moving stairs to the car-rental office, find our car, load the trunk with our bags, and set off for our house, two and a half hours away.

"Where are we?" Scott asks at every turn. "What country are we in?" Despite the signs in Italian, the red tile roofs of the villages, the distinctive landscape, he can't seem to grasp that we're in Italy, even with all the time we've logged here together over the decades, beginning with our honeymoon. "The *real* Italy? The *real* Tuscany?" he keeps repeating in amazed delight, as if he can't believe his good fortune.

At last we turn up a narrow road toward a large stone house perched at the top of a high hill. The dirt drive is adorned with a line of vibrant yellow acacia trees in full spring blossom.

"Will you just look at that yellow!" cries Scott.

"Yes," says Heather. "And they belong to our villa."

"Really? They're ours?" He grins with incredulous joy. Beginning with the Cleveland arboretum, where he first kissed me in 1950 beneath the spreading branches of that Ohio buckeye, and on to the renowned botanical gardens of Miami, Sydney, Honolulu, Tucson, and Brooklyn (with, respectively, their splendid Chinese torture, jacaranda, cannonball, saguaro, and flowering cherry trees), to the famous bo trees and banyans of India, Scott and I, ardent arbor enthusiasts, have basked in and under distinguished trees.

Norm parks the car. While Becca entertains Scott in the

living room I carry our bags upstairs, where there are two nearly identical suites, each with a queen-size bed and a bathroom, one for each couple. Downstairs, between the living room and kitchen, is another small bathroom and a study, where Becca will sleep. From our bedroom window I look past the terrace below, where we'll take our breakfast alfresco, to a distant landscape of gentle spring-green hills falling away in all directions, where the sheep that produce the famous pecorino cheeses of the province graze under the stern command of yapping dogs. As I take in all this tranquillity, I pray to the atheist god of luck that nothing will go wrong.

After our bags are unpacked, I walk across the hall to knock on Heather and Norm's door. When I open it, Heather is sobbing in Norm's arms.

"What is it?" I cry.

Heather shakes her head, tears streaming from her eyes.

"What?"

Sheepishly she says, "It's Scott. And you."

Now it's my arms that enfold and console her. I'm so used to him, to us, that I've forgotten how helpless, even tragic, we appear. To me his confusion and disorientation are such old news that what I focus on is his delight at traveling again.

"Don't cry," I say. "He's not unhappy. And I'm not either. Can't you see that?"

"Yes," she says, sniffling, "I do see it. It's amazing. But still . . ."

I tell her about several new books on happiness that report the good news about the tendency of our species to recover fairly quickly from traumatic events and revert to the mean. I tell her about the studies these books describe, showing that the disabled and chronically ill are generally no less happy than anyone else, though most people refuse to believe it. The studies reveal that most of us are not very good at predicting how we'd feel in other circumstances. Most of us say we'd rather die than be seriously impaired, though when the moment comes, most disabled people treasure their lives and do everything possible to preserve them. "Don't you see? We're fine. We're here in Tuscany. With you. What could be better?"

Scott's confusion accompanies us everywhere. But though he continues to doubt the reality of where we are, soon that veteran traveler is in his element. He plunges headfirst into relishing the landscape, the villages and towns, the art, the food, the company, and especially those vibrant yellow trees, which his extreme lack of memory keeps as fresh as if each sighting were the first. "Come over here, dearest, when you have a minute. I want to show you something marvelous out the window. Just look at that yellow tree. Isn't it incredible?" Nothing, not car sickness, fatigue, nor disorientation, impedes his continual delight. And indeed, with no decisions forced on him, with Norm as driver, Heather and me as cooks, and Becca as personal attendant, what's not to enjoy? If he's often impatient to leave the restaurant or museum before the rest of us are ready, he expresses it charmingly, urging us to "move-on-dot-com!" or, as he would never have done before his fall, bursting into improvised full-voiced song, like someone who's had too much to drink:

> Oh dear, oh dear, oh dear
> When are we going to leave here?
> I fear, I fear, I fear
> We'll never get out of here!

It's not that his old self has been supplanted, only that a new layer, less inhibited and more impatient, has been superimposed. And since the new layer is the showy one, it's the one that commands attention. But to those of us who know him well, it's clear that underneath it's still Scott, shaky but intact, the tall, sweet, blue-eyed guy who loves—has always loved—traveling.

Becca is captivated by him, as women have always been. Back when he was an iceman in his teens, making early-morning deliveries to apartment houses in downtown Cleveland, some customers regularly waited for him in their negligees to take him into their beds. "Today he told me he used to play the accordion, on top of everything else. Is that true?" asks Becca breathlessly. I confirm that as a boy he played in an all-accordion band that rehearsed every Saturday at the May Company on Cleveland's Public Square. "He is just the sweetest man," she whispers while he's in the bathroom. "Did you hear him a minute ago? He really had to go bad, but even so, he asked me if I wanted to use the bathroom first. Has he always been like that?"

"Yes, always," I say, grateful that his injury, which damaged so much, left his sweetness unimpaired, even if sometimes overwhelmed by anger or frustration.

When his impatience threatens to disrupt our plans, Becca takes him by the hand to a garden or yet another café to sit and talk until the rest of us are ready to join them. Otherwise he and I are seldom apart. Since his fall I have never seen him so continually joyful, so little agitated—which makes me declare the trip a complete success.

We arrive back in New York at midnight. The next day, after a long sleep, Scott wakes up saying excitedly, "We forgot to bring something home from Tuscany. Something very important."

"We did? What?" I ask, astounded that he remembers the trip at all.

"A yellow tree!"

That he remembers our having been in Tuscany is astonishing enough; that he remembers the acacia trees seems nothing short of miraculous. His artist's eye has brought home across an ocean, from the past to the present, at least one vivid image in living color. To me it marks a turning point, a milestone of recall and recovery. I can barely contain my excitement.

After Heather e-mails us her photos of the trip, he can't stop looking at them. I put up an image of red tile roofs, taken from the highest point of the village, as a screensaver on my computer desktop; then I order prints of all the photos and mount them in an album, which immediately becomes his favorite book. He looks at it endlessly, commenting on each image. A few weeks later, looking at the album, he crows, "What a trip that was! I seem to have come out of my shell on that trip. Glorious photos! Wonderful trip!" The pictures spark other memories of things of which there are no photos, like Norm's speeding up and down the hills, the grazing sheep, the dogs barking at their heels.

With Karin's urging and help, Scott makes two pastel drawings of the yellow trees, using the photos as inspiration. And for many months, whenever we see Norm and Heather, he asks them if one day we can all go back to Tuscany. His memory of the adventure has successfully made the leap from short-term to long-term, where it now resides. Is this tremendous achievement a result of ordinary healing over time (now approaching two years), or perhaps of his intense, unexpected pleasure, rendering it unforgettable?

Little is known about the way information in your short-term memory—like the name of the person you just met or the whereabouts of the book you were just reading—is converted into long-term memory for retrieval whenever you want it, be it hours or years later. A memory is a set of neural connections among brain cells, but whether a given set of connections is made permanent often depends upon emotions; otherwise you wouldn't fixate forever on a particularly embarrassing moment or remember the face of your rival longer than that of your waiter.

Sometimes the failure to remember an experience occurs because it can't be retrieved and sometimes because it was not properly encoded in the first place. Experiments have shown that memory traces, which start as stimuli from sources outside the brain, are initially encoded in the sensory cortex. Each repetition of the image or sound reinforces the brain's complex neural network until, after enough repetition and neural restimulation, the words and images become eligible for the process of conversion to long-term memories. (Though not, evidently, for the demented, whose ceaseless repetitions are forgotten as soon as they are uttered.) If consolidation of short-term into long-term memory does not get under way quickly, the data are simply lost.

Mapping of brain activity through advanced imaging techniques has established that the hippocampi, important structures deep inside the temporal lobes, are critical to the process of making memories stick, but how it works is not understood. Neuroscientists, conducting experiments on slugs, rats, and monkeys, have established connections between memory retention and, variously, a certain gene, a particular enzyme, REM sleep patterns, a molecular pathway, a habit state. But how memories are actually laid down and stored in the brain—what the process of becoming electrochemically hardwired consists of—remains a mystery.

Indeed, since memories of different kinds of things (colors, numbers, music, places, faces, names, among many others) are "stored" in different specific areas of the brain and can be altered over time with subsequent recollections, the generalized concepts of long-term and short-term memory are no more than theoretical constructs—as is that of the even briefer "immediate" memory (also called "working" or "running"), which lasts for only a moment or two, like the phone number you just looked up that disappears as soon as you've dialed it. Cognitive scientists disagree as to how many kinds of memory systems there are, and they often divide memory into ever finer categories, including sensory memory (input from the senses), procedural memory (of skills and habits, such as tying your shoes or playing the violin), semantic memory (of the facts that make up our general knowledge of the world, as opposed to our personal experience of it, such as the fact that the earth circles the sun or that pollution causes global warming), episodic memory (of events that occurred to us in a specific time and place), associative memory (which can connect the taste of a madeleine, for example, with a flood of feelings from the past), and more. Suffice it to say that people with head injuries and other neural impairments almost always have considerable, often disabling, difficulty both encoding and retrieving information of many sorts—which makes Scott's ongoing recall of our Tuscan adventure all the more remarkable.

Thinking back on that trip, undertaken as a risky experiment, I am surprised to discover that for me too it was no less gratifying than many another. With Becca along to cover for me, I did nearly everything I wanted. It also marks a turning point. All travel can expand one's horizons, but this trip has set a precedent for us by stretching the limits of what's possible to do with the new, impaired Scott, at least for now, given the right friends, the right assistance, and the right preparations. Its success emboldens me to think about climbing back on the horse by returning to the nubble come summer, despite the primitive facilities—perhaps in time to defiantly celebrate the second anniversary of his miraculous survival.

❦

We've barely adjusted to being home when suddenly Karin announces she is moving back to Texas in July. There goes our vaunted stability.

This disruption couldn't have come at a worse time, because

I finally have a publishing contract for this very book, and with it a deadline. I throw myself headlong into the search for Karin's replacement, hoping to find someone before she leaves. But with the students on summer break, no one responds to my postings. By fall they'll be scrambling to find places to live and part-time jobs, but for now the last thing on their minds is next term's housing. I expand my base, ask everyone I know for leads, and follow up on each one, no matter how unpromising. But July arrives, Karin leaves, and still I have no one.

Since abandoning my single-minded, all-absorbing calling of healing Scott, which buoyed me for over a year, the minimal conditions I now require to keep my spirit alive are

> to be able to cook a meal without steady interference;
> to be free to read without constant interruption;
> to work on my writing every day.

As long as I'm caring for him round the clock, I have none of these, not one, and I soon begin to sink. It seems that he always manages to intrude on me in the kitchen at precisely the critical moment or scuttle my reading just as the scene or argument reaches its climax. Those behaviors that I was able to take in stride when I had five hours to renew myself each day—his asking the same question a dozen times, exploding when I try to correct him, elbowing pedestrians who walk too close, unplugging the lamps from the walls instead of turning off the switches, insisting that we are in London and must try to get home—now push me over the edge. Our self-assertion leads to strife that begins with my irritation ("Won't you please stay out of the kitchen while I'm cooking?") and ends with his shouting at the top of his lungs ("All right, I'm GONE! You'll never see me again for the rest of my LIFE!" kicking a table as he storms from the room). I know I must *prevent a crisis before it starts*, but I can't be better than I am or do more than I can do.

One evening, after weeks of my caring for him without relief has exhausted us both to the breaking point, during a minor spat he suddenly roars, grabs both my arms, backs me against the wall, and spits in my face, leaving me shaken by fear and rage. Breaking my own taboo, I say the unspeakable: I threaten to put him in a nursing home. In response he picks up a chair as if to hurl it at me, and I do the unthinkable—I call 911. "Okay, now the police will come and take you away," I say in my fury.

As we wait for them, I wonder who is slave and who master, who the abuser and who the abused, which of us is the more aggressive and which the more pathetic. The shock of what's happened immediately calms him, so that by the time four giant police, three men and a woman, stride through our door, we seem like a courteous old couple living in quiet harmony.

"Come in, come in, come in," says the expansive host, waving them toward the sofas. "How are you tonight?"

They stand near the entrance, looking around at our well-ordered loft, puzzled. "Is there anyone else here?" asks the lead cop.

"No-o-o-o," I reply, as if I had no idea why they've come. Embarrassed to have called them, I feel suddenly protective of Scott. Though these days he often leaves me feeling battered, my power is great, his small.

"What seems to be the trouble?"

I offer a quick description of Scott's TBI and assure them that our little crisis has passed. "I'm so sorry I bothered you."

Again, puzzlement. They huddle, confer.

"Was he ever violent before his . . . accident?" asks one.

"Oh, never," I say. "He was the soul of gentleness."

"Then you might want to try hypnosis," he says, as if brain damage were a habit to be broken, like smoking.

"Well, we're always here if you need us," offers the lead cop, and precedes the other giants to the door.

The minute they're gone, Scott forgets they were here, and we walk toward our bed hand in hand to watch a movie. United, relieved, and for the moment saved.

Now desperate for help, I place my hopes on one of our occasional evening Scott Watchers, who really wants that next-door loft. Ginny, who has just graduated from NYU in film studies, is probably too young and inexperienced to handle the job. It's one thing of an evening to eat ice cream and watch basketball with him at home when I'm due back shortly; it's quite another to think up ways of keeping him engaged for hours on end away from home. But who else is there? To prepare Ginny for the worst I give her a copy of "Coping and Caring Techniques for Caregivers," lend her *The 36-Hour Day*, recommend the online *TBI Survival Guide* (TBIguide.com), and offer her a trial run at the job.

The first day, he goes off with her willingly enough, but after an hour I hear him yelling in the hall. He can accelerate from calm to agitated like a Nascar champ. The next day she arrives an hour late. More intermittent screaming. The third day she fails to show up at all, and I never see her again.

Our doctor suggests that I try experienced professionals instead of students. Though I'm skeptical, given our prior failures with agency aides, I place my hopes in a friend of Scott's former aide Big Barbara, who has fifteen years' experience working with dementia patients. But she too quits after her second day, overwhelmed by his shouting and cursing. Sorry to have let me down, she has a white moth orchid (*Phalaenopsis*), with a jaunty round face like hers, delivered to us the next day.

It withers in a week from my ignorant, overzealous watering.

As the weeks pass, with one failed prospect after another, my life begins to unravel. Each defeat pushes me closer to despair. *You must allow time for yourself. Respite is essential,* counsels "Coping and Caring Techniques for Caregivers," without offering tips on how to find it. I become so demoralized that I find myself again bursting into tears at unpredictable moments. Scott is shaken. "Don't cry, dearest, you'll hurt your eyes," he says, trying to comfort me. But I'm unable to stop. "Please . . . please. I'll do anything to help you not cry . . . What can I do?" Gently stroking my hair, he vows aloud not to drive away another Scott Watcher—as if he could control his behavior by an act of will or could remember why I'm crying. The futility of his good intentions only makes our predicament feel more hopeless.

As I sink deeper into despondency under weeks of unrelenting caregiving, I begin to wonder if the time has finally come to consider the hitherto unthinkable and look for a nursing home.

A nursing home!

By entertaining that option, with one stroke I nullify the purpose of my last two years. Yet no matter how I parse our predicament and survey my choices, it keeps reverting to a question of self-preservation. It's him or me now. His life or mine.

"I can't go on doing this," I begin to say to anyone who will listen.

"Of course you can't!" cries Linda. "Twenty-four/seven is totally unacceptable. You must have your five hours a day alone as an absolute minimum. You must be able to do your work. Otherwise how will you manage to keep your love alive, much less your spirit? No one could survive doing what you do."

Heather points out that if I fall apart, so will Scott.

Polly agrees. "You can't keep this up, Mom. You've done it for too long already. You know that a nursing home is inevitable eventually—you'll just have to do it sooner rather than later. You must have your life back."

Our doctor (handing me a box of tissues as I go to pieces in his office while Scott sits quietly in the waiting room) says, "I know you've been against it, but maybe it's time to consider drugs for him"—meaning the antipsychotic drugs that are used in low doses to control agitation in the elderly demented, the very drugs the fancy neurology consultant took him off of when he was at Rusk. Delicately, our doctor reminds me that Scott and I have often talked about our end-of-life choices, insisting that burdening each other is an unacceptable option. "You and I both know how he felt when his mind was intact. You've both made your wishes clear to me on many occasions. His advanced directives are right here in his chart."

Death—his, mine—suddenly seems sweet. I keep hearing in my ears Scott's answer to the trauma doctor's candid question about whether he'd want to be kept alive if he couldn't continue to live independently: *No, I don't think so. No.* I read over the stark words of our living wills: *If I am irreversibly demented . . . withhold all treatments or interventions which are not designed solely for my comfort.*

The next day, Scott confirms his choice. We've been talking again about the fact that each Scott Watcher since Karin has quit on the second day. "I love you, my darling, you know it, but I can't do this anymore, it's too much for me," I tell him tearfully.

"I agree. You can't. And I don't want you to. You know that, don't you?"

"I do."

"Then what will you do? Put me in the old-age home?"

"Do you know of any other options?"

"Get a gun and shoot myself"—his agitated refrain.

"You mean you'd rather be dead than in a nursing home?"

"Yes."

I'm so taken aback by his answer that I ask again. And again he says, "Yes," but this time he tacks on, as a hedge, "I don't know what it's like in a nursing home."

A few minutes later I hear him moaning on the sofa.

"What's the matter? Why are you moaning?"

"Because I have no future."

I rush to comfort him, kissing his hands, his face, horrified to have passed my hopelessness on to him.

"Thank you," he says, stroking my cheek. Then: "It's like being in a lifeboat together, isn't it? We have to take care of each other."

"Yes."

"It's a deal?"

"Deal."

"Shake on it?"

We shake.

Increasingly desperate, I'm willing to try anything. If drugs will keep him calm, I'm ready to use them. We visit the nearby adult day-care center, a facility specializing in activities for the physically and cognitively impaired, suggested by our doctor, conveniently situated only three blocks from our loft. With me beside him Scott enjoys the tour of the facility and agrees to give it a try. Tentatively hopeful again, I begin the long application process and while I'm at it also send for applications to two recommended nursing homes (reminding myself that I needn't yet fill them out)—anything to keep me actively seeking a solution, my antidote to despair.

A geriatric social worker whom a friend recommends for her savvy and her network assures me that I'm wrong to consider my situation hopeless; it's only a matter of finding the right person.

"But he drives away everyone I hire with his screaming and cursing. They all quit after the second day."

"He doesn't curse at his friends, does he? I bet he doesn't scream when he's with his family."

It's true. When my children or friends do a turn at Scott Watching, he's a lamb, never mind that he shouts and curses at me.

"So you see? It's not everyone. No, you just have to be patient until you find the right person. Wait till the end of August, when the students are back in town."

She speaks of him not as a problem, but as a person, one with tastes, preferences, and desires. My relief and gratitude for her advice are enough to shore up my fraying sanity and restore a modicum of hope. In this dead time of oppressive heat, when I'm not free to write and there's no one to hire, I book airline tickets for Maine, in time for the second anniversary of his fall, in hopes that a change of scene may somehow make things right again.

EIGHT

Nubble

If caring for Scott around the clock was hard when we were home in the city, it's impossible on the island. Our stairs to and from the beach are too steep and rickety for his safety; the gaslights are too complicated for him to light; the outhouse takes too long to get to; he can't negotiate the steps at night, and in the daytime, since the nubble shore is hazardously rocky, the only place safe enough for him to walk is back and forth across the beach.

Once again Heather and Norm come to our rescue by inviting us to spend our nights in their basement guest room. Unlike our own house on the nubble, theirs has electric lights, and a bathroom just for us, with a flush toilet and hot shower. We can sleep there at night and, during the days, while they're at work on their computers (she writing a dissertation, he running a New York office), walk out to the nubble, where Scott can scream and curse all he likes: there'll be no one around to hear.

His disorientation has never been greater. On the ferry from Portland, he kept asking when the boat would get to Europe, and now, at the end of our first day in the house where he visited me several times each summer for twenty years, he wakes from a nap asking me, "Are you my mother or my wife?"

I'm flabbergasted. His mother has been dead for three decades. Not since his hospital days has he betrayed such confusion. Is it because the sundowning hour is approaching? Because we've returned to the scene of the crime? Because I'm older than she was when she died? Because I'm the one who cares for him?

"Your wife, my darling. I'm your wife." Still, his perplexity does make a kind of sense. My caring for him is not so different from mothering a young child—I oversee his meals and schedule, his medications and hygiene, reminding him to brush his teeth, floss, wash, pee, wipe. I manage his schedule, set up doctors' appointments and playdates, transport him, arrange for sitters. I track his possessions, launder his clothes, help him dress and undress, guide him through traffic, answer his questions, interpret the world. I think up ways to stimulate him and supervise his activities. Like a mother, I worry about him, discipline him, run interference for him, extricate him from trouble, protect him, defend him, comfort him, love him.

"But you've never been here before, have you?" he asks, puzzled.

"Only every summer for forty years."

"But not with me—we've never been in this place together before, have we?"

Does he now think I'm his mother, who has never been here? By way of answer, I sit him down at the big table and recite the entire story of our island romance, from his first visit here in 1984 until now, twenty-two years later. He listens rapt, like a child hearing the treasured story of his birth, as I remind him of the first night he slept in this house: after a dinner of lobster and wild food, reluctant to overstay his welcome, he decided to leave on the last ferry rather than accept my belated invitation to spend the night, and he made me trail him halfway across the island practically begging him to return to the nubble. "I chased you all the way to the first streetlight at the top of the hill, where the dirt road ends, remember? That was it for me. By the time we got to the top of the hill, I was really mad. The only reason I could imagine that you wanted to leave instead of staying the night was that you had a date on the mainland with another woman. If you hadn't turned around and followed me home, that would have been the end."

He squeezes my hand and says, "There has never been another woman. Never!" As there was never, for me, another man, after he returned to my life.

I'd begun to recount our story in an attempt to reorient him, but now I'm telling it for my sake too. "And the next morning," I continue, "we sat on a log down on the beach, facing the ocean, trying to bare our hearts—only you didn't know how, remember? Instead of telling me about your life and your feelings, you told me about every mountain you ever climbed. You were so touching and sweet and beautiful that I loved you anyway."

I take his hand and lead him around the house to point out each improvement he's made over the years using nothing but hand tools and muscle. I show him the photo of him as a handsome youth that I keep on my desk, the picture postcards tacked on the wall that he mailed to me from Italy and New York, and the gifts he's brought me here over the years on his many visits. Through the window I show him the solar panels on the studio roof he once gave me for my birthday as part of his grand scheme to help me in my work, and the studio itself, which, to ensure my privacy, he had earlier designed for me and built from scratch—where, exactly two years ago, he fell to the floor, changing our lives forever.

Returning from my own reverie, I watch him struggle to comprehend. He asks, "And what would you be doing now if I hadn't fallen?"

"I'd be writing in the studio."

His face looks solemn, taking it in. "And what would I be doing?"

"You'd be in here in the house reading or outdoors working on a project."

He shakes his head. "This is all completely mind-boggling, because though I don't doubt that *I've* been here before, I don't remember ever coming here with *you*—not even on this particular visit we're having right now this minute. Isn't this weird?"

"No, not weird, just that your injury has made you disoriented."

He spreads his hands in bewilderment. "I can remember the water lapping the beach, the waves, the sky turning orange, that house over there on the far side of the cove with the big windows—they're all very familiar. But what completely confuses me is that you're here with me. Don't get me wrong, I'm glad you're here, I find it delightful—you know that, don't you? But I can't remember your ever being here before."

"I've been coming here twice as long as you have."

Then, with an expression of pained puzzlement, he asks, "Do you mind if I ask you something?"

"Please."

"Are you my mother or my wife?"

With nothing for him to do here anymore, no art, no reading, no building projects, no clearing of underbrush or overgrowth, no wood chopping, no walks on the rocks or mucking around in the tidal pools, he is condemned to idleness. In his boredom and confusion his agitation increases, and with it, mine. This nubble, once my haven of solitude, is useless to me now. Since he can't be left alone, whatever is out-of-bounds for him is also out-of-bounds for me, which rules out everything I've loved here: I can't wander over the rocks to collect wild greens, can't go down to the cove for shellfish, can't wade in the water or check the apples on my tree, and worst of all, I can't think or meditate or write or even read. I try to give him simple kitchen tasks to do, but with his abridged attention span he quickly tires of them, and the days are long.

On my birthday he takes a long morning nap, giving me the best possible gift: a full hour and a half alone. Reading a friend's manuscript to the throbbing music of the surf, I feel like myself again, in tune with everything around me.

Until he wakes and it's over. When I ask him if he'll please wait just till I finish the chapter, he readily agrees, but with his damaged sense of time he immediately begins to pace like a caged animal, fixated on leaving the house. "Just a little longer," I plead—"It's my birthday, please do this for me." Again, supportive as always, he agrees. I've often been able to gain some time by reminding him of his long-standing desire to enable my work. But this time he can't control his impatience; soon he is storming around the room growling, then shouting, "How long do you intend to read? Are you going to read all day? What about *me*?" and he threatens to leave the house by himself.

"Do whatever you want!" I snarl, and scooping up the pages, I head for the studio, determined to claim a few more minutes of privacy no matter what. Let him tumble down the stairs and die!

He follows me as far as the outhouse, where he stops to pee, but unable to let me out of his sight, he returns not to the house but to the studio. Overflowing with apologies, he takes me in his arms and promises to "do better," and for a few minutes he lies quietly on the bed (which Polly and Andrew, on an earlier visit, have moved downstairs for us) while I finish reading the chapter. When I stop, harmony reigns again.

We walk to the Spar, the island's only restaurant, for lunch. It's a clear, blue, breezy summer day. Eating clams and fries on the deck, watching the sailboats and fishing boats and ferries, we are completely happy. He takes my hand across the table and says, "Of all the women I ever traveled with, you are the best companion. I'm so lucky to be married to you." As we leave the Spar, he looks down and says, "Damn! My shoelace is untied." I rush to the ground to tie it before he can imperil his shaky balance by bending over, only to find the laces perfectly tied. "Ha! You went for the fake!" he shouts gleefully, playful as a child. On the way home, we stop to say hello to Pammy at the post office, Lorinda at the store, Nancy at the library, all of whom are thrilled to see this walking miracle putting on the charm. He even displays cognitive improvement, referring correctly to the time of day as late afternoon. I stop in amazement. "How do you know that?" I ask. "What?" "That it's late afternoon." "By the shadows on the pavement, of course."

But the next day the nightmare returns. While I'm at the outhouse, he leaves the house by himself. Finding him missing, I'm frantic, until I deduce that since there's nowhere else he can go, he must have returned to Heather and Norm's, and then I'm mortified that these friends, who have been so kind to us, will have to drop what they're doing to bring him home.

Afraid to go after him in case I've guessed wrong, I stand on the deck scanning the beach through binoculars. After some time I spot three figures walking slowly toward the nubble, one of them stooped like Scott.

From then on, I must wage a long, continuous struggle to keep him from bothering our hosts. The thought of their work interrupted appalls me; he's my responsibility, not theirs. I plead, threaten, forbid; when he insists on going there anyway, I have no choice but to follow him down the stairs and across the beach, trying to talk him out of disturbing them. As I alternate reasons and pleas, he responds by throwing curses and sticks. Unable to understand why I want him not to disturb them, he threatens to punch me in the face, stomp on my bare feet, push me down unless I go away. Fortunately, at this state of the tide, the beach is wide enough for me to keep my distance.

Not that I'm really afraid. Deep down I know that this basically gentle, loving man would never hurt me, know that his rage is at his condition, not at me. Still, I'm dismayed by how badly he's deteriorated in our few days here, making him sound like the kind of man he most abhors and would be ashamed to resemble if he knew: a wife abuser.

Switching to bribery, I finally calm him down by offering to take him across the island to the store for an ice-cream cone. He immediately forgets about Heather and Norm, even as we pass their house. "You are the best mom. You take such good care of me," he says as we trudge up the hill and then asks sheepishly, "Have I been a bad boy?"

At the store, licking his cone, he asks again, "Are you my mother or my wife?"

"I'm your wife. I wonder why you've suddenly become so confused about this."

"Oh, don't worry about it," he says cavalierly, waving a hand. "It's just a brain thing." He holds up his hand and starts crossing and uncrossing his middle finger over his index finger—"Like this. They keep switching back and forth: mother and wife. Just a brain thing, that's all"—explained with all the self-assurance of any normal, knowing adult.

❦

Mary, a friend of Heather and Norm's, who over the years of being their frequent houseguest has also become my friend, walks out to the nubble for afternoon tea with Scott and me.

Sometimes he amuses us with endearing non sequiturs and surprising turns of mind, but just as often, unable to follow our
conversation, he interrupts by loudly saying "What's next?" or
"Can't we move on?"—bringing everything to a halt.

When he goes to the outhouse, Mary says, "Have you always been so patient? You have the patience of a saint!" and dismisses my demurrals as mere modesty, further evidence of my
virtue.

If she only knew! Does a saint call out the cops? How stack
up my patient moments against the ones when I'm irritated or
resentful? Those who see me as saintly assume that I've sacri-
ficed my life for him, as a saint sacrifices hers for Christ. But I
haven't—nor could I, nor would I. As long as I can work and
think, I have my life.

Over these past two years I've become convinced that the
frequent allegation of saintliness actually has little to do with
me. Rather, that quality, like beauty, is in the eye of the beholder, whose own terrified recoil from my situation (there but
for the grace of god . . .) requires that she distance herself cat-
egorically from me. If I am a saint, then she, an ordinary mortal unlike me, cannot be expected, even in fantasy, to sacrifice
her freedom to care for a demented loved one (whose one-
dimensional diminishment is also in the eye of the beholder). If
I am a saint, I can be dismissed as an exception, but if I am
not, I stand as a living accusation, a challenge, a threat. "Are you
trying to be some kind of hero?" sneered one cynical acquain-
tance, "or is this just *love*?"—as if I were faking it, as Camus de-
scribes in *The Fall*: "Modesty helped me to shine, humility to
conquer, and virtue to oppress." But willingly caring for Scott,
the mere doing of which constitutes my so-called heroism,
can't be faked.

When my children were growing up I remember feeling
something similar about the parents of disabled children, whose

"sacrifice" seemed so horrendous that only a saint or hero would take it on, but whose choice to do so (if it can be called a "choice") I now understand: it's the contract and consolation of love.

After Mary leaves, I try to read again, but finding it futile, I complain to Scott wearily about his incessant interruptions. Suddenly he stands up, pounds on the table, and in a fierce display of devotion protests passionately, "This is *not* what I want or have ever wanted. It's so unfair! You *must* have time to read. You must!" Then, turning abruptly gentle, he adds, "You are so good to me. You make my whole life worthwhile. How can I ever pay you back?"

"You can't pay me back," I answer, invoking again the wedding vows. "Anyway," I quip, "you've already paid me—in advance."

"But . . . are you happy?"—assuming, as he always has, the burden of my happiness.

"Happy enough," I reassure him, "as long as I get my time alone. And you?"

"As long as I'm with my honey."

And there it is, the paradox of our predicament. The relentlessness of his needs and the frustration of mine are one. Neither of us a sinner, neither a saint.

Island friends, Lynn and Tim, ask me if I will take their preteen daughters and their neighbor's children around the nubble for a refresher course on how to find and identify the edible wild greens, seaweeds, and shellfish I used to thrive on here and a decade ago wrote a book about. Lynn, once an occupational therapist who specialized in brain injury, offers to stay up in the house with Scott while I give the tour. When I warn her about the agitation that now overtakes him whenever I'm out of his sight, she points out that from the deck they'll be able to see us down on the rocks. "If it gets to be a problem, I'll holler and you can come back up."

She tells me the good news that when she worked with the brain injured, she was taught that agitation is a sign of increased brain activity. And it's true that as his fog lifts and his reactions intensify, his agitation does sometimes seem to increase.

"Not that it makes him any easier to live with, I grant you," she says. "But it is an improvement. He's probably entered a new stage."

If it's true, I wonder what this next stage will hold. As his TBI continues to improve and his earlier dementia continues its inevitable downhill slide, will the next stage be better or worse? As always, there's nothing to do but wait and see.

We set a date for the tour on the day and hour of lowest tide, just after the full moon, when the tidal pools are most exposed. So it is that for the first time in three years I'm able again to gather my wild greens, visit my seaweed garden, and, by upending rocks or quickly tossing aside handfuls of rockweed, uncover the small green crabs that the children help me collect in a sand pail. Snacking on seaweed—the crunchy arame and salty sea lettuce—as we tour the nubble, I feel old age pour off of me into the all-absorbing ocean, until I am suddenly carefree and light.

Back at the house, I sauté the crabs for lunch and also cook lentils with sea rocket, kelp, garlic, chopped wild sorrel, and a dash of balsamic vinegar. I serve them on the deck with an orache-and-dandelion salad, feeling elated and accomplished again, as I did before the accident.

How little it takes to lift my spirits and restore my equanimity! Someone to spell me with Scott whom he accepts and I trust, a walk along the shore, a meal I can cook with imagination and freedom, and I am myself again.

We're returning to New York on Thursday, Mary's leaving to-morrow, and Heather and Norm are hosting a farewell dinner. I've saved for tonight the jar of truffle paste I bought in Tuscany and brought to the island as a gift for them. We plan to use it on tonight's fettuccine (with lobster, scallops, and clams).

Just as Heather is about to drop the pasta into the pot of boiling water, I realize that I've forgotten to bring over the truffle paste. "Wait!" I shout, just in time. Leaving Scott in their care, I take off across South Beach toward the nubble.

With dusk approaching, everyone has left the beach. The only sounds are the screech and twitter of shorebirds and the waves hitting the shore. The tide is out, the beach is wide. I run across it swiftly, my feet scarcely touching the ground. I cross over the low dunes to the nubble, fly up the stairs to our house, grab the truffle paste, then run down the stairs and back over to South Beach, where I jog across the sand—my first such jog in three years, since the summer before the accident. I breathe in the salt air through my widened nostrils, taking in the smells of iodine, seaweed, and salt. The blue sky has begun to streak with swaths of pink and red and green, all reflected on the sur-face of the water. Gulls glide and swoop on the air currents, a flock of sandpipers run along the edge of the shore slightly ahead of me, then rise as one and turn in unison to land again farther up the beach—and suddenly I feel as buoyant and free as I've ever felt before. Free as a child in summer, free as a girl who has finally left home, free as a mother whose children have gone away, free as a wife whose husband is off to a conference, free as a kite that has broken loose, free as a bird riding the wind.

Then I walk in the door.

"There you are!" cries Scott, coming toward me with his arms spread. "Finally! I was afraid you'd been kidnapped."

"You see? I told you she'd be back, didn't I?" says Heather triumphantly.

"Yes, you did. But I don't trust anyone. You can't count on anything."

Sometimes I try to imagine other outcomes of that accident: If he had recovered enough to be reasonably independent. If he had been able to continue making art. If he had gone mad and had to be locked away. If I had sent him to a nursing home. If I had refused the respirator or "pulled the plug." If he had died in his sleep.

Then he would have been cremated, his ashes divided between his daughter and the ocean off the nubble. And I would have launched another life.

This thought alternately inspires and torments me. No more daily bondage, no more unrelenting responsibility. But at the same time, no ballast, no purpose, no love. Which would I be, light as the air or heavy as a gravestone? Giddily free or unbearably bereft?

Forget it—he's alive, he is mine, and I am his.

Back in New York I renew my search for the right person to replace Karin. Two more students give it a try, but neither one can take the stress. Desperate for relief from giving round-the-clock care, I enroll Scott at the adult day-care center three blocks up Seventh Avenue. It's like dropping a reluctant child at nursery school, only worse: he has no idea who all those decrepit people are or why he's among them. When I explain that he's there to give me some respite from caring for him full-time so I can work, he rushes to assure me that he's all for it, but moments after I depart, he's forgotten everything and tries to leave, setting off piercing alarms every time he opens the door. When the staff stops him, he reacts with rage. On his third visit he holds an umbrella, stiff-armed, and whirls around, clearing a protective circle. Every day he's there, the director calls me at home (where I know better than to try to work) to ask me to come get him. At her insistence, each day before I drop him off I give him a dose of the antiagitation drug prescribed by his doctor, but it doesn't help, and when the two-week trial is up, I am notified that he is "not fitting in" and won't be welcome back.

Now I wonder if that experience, or perhaps the medication, might have had adverse effects, because the strange phenomenon called sundowning, so long quiescent, looms again over our lives. When Scott first fell under its sway, I understood it as an aspect of hospital life, where the obliteration of night and day interferes with the body's circadian rhythms, an explanation confirmed by the disappearance of the symptoms after his discharge. But now I read that sundowning is also a common affliction of people with dementia, who suffer increased confusion and agitation in the late afternoon and evening, when (according to the Alzheimer's Association) "they may become demanding, suspicious, upset or disoriented, see or hear things that are not there [hallucinations] or believe things that are not true [delusions]."

Scott is now seized by a delusion every afternoon around five o'clock, when he begins to insist that we go "home."

"But we *are* home," I explain.

"I mean home to our other house, over there," he says, pointing out the windows to the west. This obsession grips him daily for several hours, right up to the moment we sit down to eat our dinner. "Can't you please get your car and take me to the other house?" he asks, no matter how often I assure him that we have no other house and don't own a car. "If you won't drive me, then let's walk there. *Right now!*"

No one knows what causes sundowning with dementia,

though there is no absence of theories: the decreased light and
lengthening shadows of dusk that affect the body's internal
clock, the flurry of new household activities inaugurated at that
hour, fatigue, the physical memory of going home at close of
day. Scott's particular obsession with another house reminds me
of a recurring dream I had for many years, a dream I assume
must be primal, of a vast, calm, secret space that lies behind my
bedroom, an entire other apartment, which soothes and comforts me. It reminds me too of every child's joy in creating ar-
chitectural spaces—under the covers, beneath a table, in a giant
carton, inside a tent, up a tree—to serve as one's own "other
house."

Sometimes I try to reason away his delusion or argue him
out of it: "What house do you mean? Where is it?"

"You know, on Washington Boulevard, across from the
school."

"That house! You haven't lived there for sixty years! Your
family moved out when you were eighteen. It's probably gone
by now. Besides, that house was in Cleveland. We're in New
York, hundreds of miles away. Even if it exists we can't get
there." But no matter how much evidence I marshal or how
strong a case I build, he silently waits me out, then launches
again his incessant refrain.

Sometimes he tries to sweet-talk me into walking him
there; sometimes he simply heads for the door (now locked
from the inside with a key I keep hidden, contra the fire code).
Sometimes he goes so far as to grant all my contentions, as if
reason had returned ("You're right, no other house exists"),
only to take up his cause again a moment later: "Are you almost ready? We need to get there as soon as possible. Let's get
going."

I too try a variety of tactics, from logic to distraction to authority to steely silence. But all are in vain until, in the end, I

give in to his powerful delusion by conceding, "Okay, if you insist I'll take you there after dinner"—knowing that by then he will probably have forgotten about it until the next day at five, when it will all begin again.

Then, as suddenly as the life raft foundered and broke, leaving me drowning, along floats the ideal companion for Scott: Judith Bradford, a graduate student in the NYU program in arts administration, intelligent, calm, cultivated, soft-spoken, tall, slender, competent, and eager for the job. Every reference I check gives her a glowing recommendation. When I voice my fears that she may be too refined to withstand his verbal assaults, she sets her jaw and says, "Try me," and I do.

The first day goes better than either of us imagined. The second, she reports, is "even easier," and the third is the best. As an arts administration student, she has a free pass to all the museums in the city and plans to take him to a different one every day. And sure enough, each afternoon as I open the door to greet him, he wears an admission sticker on his jacket and an exuberant smile on his lips.

The social worker was right: all it takes is the right person. Who has turned up not a minute too soon, because a large new research study has exposed the meds prescribed to calm the agitated elderly—which I'd looked to as a fallback—as no better than placebos. In their place are recommended *patience* and *understanding*.

One day he comes rushing to my desk to show me a notice in the Duke alumni magazine of a new book, *The Encyclopedia of Duke Basketball*, by John Roth. "Do you think you could get this book for me?" he asks in a show of initiative so remarkable that I order it on the spot.

Two days later it arrives. "Thank you, thank you, thank

you," he keeps repeating as he immerses himself in its pages. It never occurs to him to look himself up, so I do it. "Look at this!"

> York, Scotty. A 6–0 guard from Cleveland Heights, Ohio, Scott York played on the varsity for four seasons, 1948–51, and lettered for the last three. He totaled 411 points in 98 games and was most valuable for setting up teammates for baskets . . . As a senior York started alongside [Dick] Groat and averaged 7.8 points while also serving as team captain. One of his biggest feeds that year [1950, the year of our romance!] was to Dayton Allen for the winning points in a victory over Tulane in the Dixie Classic. The Blue Devils had rallied from 32 points down to tie the score entering the final minute.

To him this entry is not particularly interesting, but to me it's an eye-opener. *Most valuable for setting up teammates for baskets* starkly reminds me of the quality I first fell for and treasure still: innocent of ego, supportive to the core—as he played and loved and lived.

In face of such a model, how can I do less? For the time being, those nursing home applications I had sent away for in my panic I banish to the dark recesses of the bottom drawer and eagerly return to work.

NINE

Amor Fati

The crisis of the summer has faded from view, like the nubble shrouded in fog. When Scott is off with Judith and I'm writing about him, my mood is tranquil, hopeful, occasionally even ecstatic, despite the sometimes grim content—and worlds away from the frustration and irritation I felt when caring for him was unrelieved and all-consuming. Writing takes me out of my sometimes beleaguered self into the trancelike realm of alpha waves, where, like Scott, I live in the moment. With five focused hours a day of aesthetic relief, I have my life again, with enough satisfaction to carry me through the entire day, and in the evenings back to the world, no longer alien. From this place of calm it seems not only useless but mean to brood on chaos or wish things other than they are.

When that tough-minded visionary philosopher Friedrich Nietzsche proposed his principle *amor fati,* love of fate—meaning " 'love your fate,' which is in fact your life"—he wasn't suggesting that you love only the pleasant parts. He himself was suffering extreme physical pain at the time. No, to embrace life fully meant to him to accept life's inevitable limitations without hiding from them, no matter what fate had in store. "*Amor fati,*" he said, is "not merely to endure necessity, still less to deny it . . . but to *love* it." Not a passive resignation, but an active embrace. He called it his "formula for greatness in a human being." *Amor fati!* Love your fate. Love what is.

My fate took a turn on July 22, 2004. Absurd it would be to hide from it or wish it away, much less to resist or rail against it, as if it could be undone by an act of my puny will. Not enough even to merely accept it. To live life fully within my limitations I must struggle with it, adapt to it, make the best of it, milk it for all I can. Love it.

("That's right! Hear, hear!" shouts Scott, sitting behind me in the cheering section on the love seat while I read him this passage off my screen.)

"I believe the work you're doing now," says my ever-generous friend Ann, "is the most important work there is. The Talmud says, *To save one life is to save the world.* I truly believe that. It's miraculous, what you've accomplished."

No miracle, given the fragility and turbulence of his existence. But Ann is right that my present life is less an impediment to my work than a fulfillment of it. The two faces of my calling, love and work, are two sides of a single coin. Heads or tails, there's hardly a time when I'm not actively thinking of—*caring* for—him. As I drift off to sleep after slipping late into bed and snuggling against him; when I open my eyes again to his brilliant, circular, sunlit painting of the cosmos; at my writing desk spinning out our story; and every moment we're together, in battle or harmony: he is my hub.

The proof is that not since my children were small and my freedom equally constricted have I written so efficiently. "In art as in everything else, one can build only upon a resisting foundation," wrote the great composer Igor Stravinsky in *The Poetics of Music.* "I shall go even further: my freedom will be so much the greater and more meaningful the more narrowly I limit my field of action and the more I surround myself with obstacles. Whatever diminishes constraint diminishes strength.

The more constraints one imposes, the more one frees oneself of the chains that shackle the spirit."

I write in the mornings; I read at night; and in between I'm with him. Within the range of my freedom I have what I need: a life of the heart and of the mind.

One Saturday, while I'm at my computer, Scott sits down near me and asks, "May I talk to you? I have something very important to say."

"Of course. What is it?"

His brow is furrowed, his voice urgent as he hesitantly begins. "I don't know what's going on in my little world inside my head. I'm losing charge of my body. I'm all screwed up. I think I'm losing my . . . I'm losing my*self*."

Startled by this rare bout of soul baring, which sounds to me more like recovering than losing his self, I pay close attention. "Go on," I say as my fingers attempt to transcribe his words.

"I feel I'm pushing too far ahead of my age. And I'll just come slam up against the wall and I won't be able to do anything."

His suffering saddens me, even though I'm sure that in some ways this sudden self-awareness represents progress. "Like what?"

"Like things I want to get done or things in the house that need doing. Like tonight, for example. I should be going out into the world, in the dark, to see if I can find something that will enable me to be wise, to have some wisdom."

Wisdom? Is *that* what he seeks whenever he heads for the door?

"Alix darling, when I sit here with you, and I see you moving ahead very intuitively and profitably with . . . with . . . that thing in front of your face."

"My computer?"

"Yes. I see that you're on top of everything in front of your face and in your brain, and I don't have that ability or those alternatives anymore. And I don't think I can do much more to help it. I'm afraid I've lost my nerve. As if I was an old man . . . and am just wasting your time and my time. I feel that I'm right on the brink of screwing things up with us."

"Don't worry about that. I love you. We're fine," I reassure him.

"I know things with you are in good shape, but I hate to put you through all of this." Abruptly, his tone changes. "I can and must do better. Like tonight, for example—I'm afraid if I go into the bedroom I might make everything worse. But I should be capable of going to bed and going to sleep."

With all the determination and muscle he can muster, he pushes himself up from the chair and slowly heads off toward our bed, exhausted by his effort to explain himself. Knowing he needs my help, I follow behind, hoping to stave off failure.

By the next day he's forgotten all about his confession. But as we stand on a street corner waiting to cross, for the first time since his fall he says, "Okay, the light changed. We can go now," and takes my elbow. When he guides me across, I feel euphoric, even though I know that by tomorrow this achievement too may be forgotten and lost. But if it happened once, perhaps he is capable of making it happen again.

❦

From the outside, in the third year since the accident, my life looks much as it did before, though I work a shorter day (or a longer one, if you include the extra thirty-six hours), and instead of cramming my chores into as brief a time as possible, I take Scott along and stretch them into an expedition—to the market, the library, the doctor, the hair salon, the occasional movie. When I go out by myself of an evening—to one of my monthly seminars or meetings, to book parties and readings, to political demonstrations or dinner with friends—the main differences from before the fall are that I hire a Scott Watcher and keep my cell phone on. But I go—in fact, hardly less nowadays than I ever did, thanks partly to Scott's enthusiastic support: "I want you to promise me you'll enjoy yourself with your buddies, have a really great time," he says as I give the Scott Watcher last-minute instructions. Lucky for us, my social and intellectual life was always centered on my women friends rather than on couples, with Scott happy to be home watching basketball while I was out. Now he watches with a Scott Watcher, enlightening her on the finer points of the game, and when he's not fretting over my absence enjoys the company. Once again, I do my morning exercises listening to the news, make weekly shopping excursions to the farmer's market or Chinatown, throw the occasional dinner party, host meetings and fundraisers at our loft—but now with Scott in attendance. We dance almost as often as before, albeit for shorter sessions. I still try to finish reading the current journals before the new issues arrive, work down the pile of mail, pay the bills, and answer my e-mail, though mostly after he's gone to sleep.

Scott's life is the one that seems to me drastically changed, even if he might not agree. When I ask him what difference his fall has made to his existence, he says bluntly, "Not much." Is this owing to "lack of insight," as the neurologists call it, a matter of cognitive deficits and general cluelessness? Or is it his way of adapting? He acknowledges matter-of-factly that he no longer makes art, but he says alternately that he doesn't miss it and that one day he'll start again. (Perhaps he really believes this, and possibly it's true, but he may be saying it just to please me.) He still explores the treasures of the city with Judith and has an active social and cultural life with me. If anything, it's richer than before he fell, between the extra movies, the free chamber music concerts on Tuesday afternoons at the New School, weekend interludes of Asian music at the nearby Rubin Museum, Sunday dance matinees at the Joyce Theater, and each new production of the tiny Amato Opera Company—all of which pipe rapturous infusions of dopamine directly into our right brains and are within walking distance of our loft. That he forgets the concert or dance the minute it's over hardly matters; even in undamaged brains sensual pleasures fade quickly. Like the flavor of an exquisite dish or the quality of a given orgasm, the sound of a particular performance, however transporting, won't ordinarily outlive the week. Whereas once I kept whole libraries in my head, nowadays I can recall only vaguely the contents of a book I read a month ago, but that doesn't diminish my passion for reading in the slightest.

Not that he's entirely unaware of the changes he's undergone; it's just that he doesn't connect them with his fall or find them tragic. Yes, it sometimes bothers him that he can't dress himself without my help, or go out alone, or work the telephone, or remember the season, month, or year, but not enough to spoil his day. "My memory isn't what it used to be," he'll sometimes say in explanation, or, "What I don't know won't hurt me"—the blessing of dementia. Like anyone, he has his ups and downs. Lying on the couch watching me bustle about, the man who once described his life as a series of challenging mountain ascents remarks admiringly, "I can't imagine what it's like to have such a robust body." And again: "I so admire your industry and focus." But sometimes, when he's in a blue mood, that same thought comes out as a lament: "You do so much, and I do nothing productive."

"Maybe that's true right now," I rush to comfort him, "but until you fell, you had a tremendously productive life. Look

around this loft at the artwork you've made. Look at that gusty
bronze *Embrace*. And your great painting of the cosmos. You've
produced a whole body of work that has a life of its own, even
if you stop making more. It exists and will go on existing long
after you. You should be proud of it."

He squeezes my hand. "Thank you, darling. You just added
a blast of good air to my bubble. But it's still a bubble, just waiting to burst."

When I'm the one who needs reassuring, he's there for me
too. One evening we are settled in our bed watching Pavarotti
in *La Bohème* on the arts network. As the opera nears its tragic
end and Mimi dies, I find that I can't stop weeping, imagin-
ing Scott's death, a death each of us has sometimes mercifully wished for. Which would be worse, I wonder, to leave
him or be left?—a question that keeps popping up like a rude
Rumpelstiltskin as we approach the inevitable end. Our family
histories suggest that I'll survive him, but how will I bear it? If
he survives me, with no one to take him in, he'll probably land
straight in a nursing home, also unbearable.

When I confess to him why I'm crying, he reaches out an
arm to comfort me, exactly as he always has. That lifelong atheist, who has always scoffed at the very mention of an afterlife
and couldn't care less what happens to his remains, now pulls
out all the stops to console me: "Don't worry, dearest, I won't
leave you. I'll pack your bags and take you with me to heaven.
What color wings would you like? Blue wings, white wings,
chartreuse wings? Any color you want, and I'll make sure they
fit correctly. I've already put out some feelers for trumpets,
seven, eight, nine, ten trumpets to welcome you when you arrive. I'll offer you my arm and escort you around, show you all
the sights. With you on my arm they won't be able to throw
me out. They'll say, 'Look at that beautiful woman,' and let us
stay." He hands me a tissue to dry my eyes. Then he kisses me

and says, "Don't be sad. You've made me so happy. I didn't know I could be so happy."

Back in his lucid days, he decided he'd rather be dead than live like this, going so far as to put it in writing. Now, having arrived here, instead he frequently proclaims how lucky he feels to be alive. I cannot doubt him, even if sometimes I fantasize about his death. He can lie on the couch for hours relishing the world outside our windows: in spring he calls me over to witness the "beautiful gray wet day"; in summer, the intricate stone carvings on the building across the street; in winter, the "incredibly magnificent snowstorm"; and in every season the reflections on our ceiling of the car windshields lit by sunlight as they pass below on Seventh Avenue, creating an ever-changing light show. "Come quickly! You have no idea what a marvelous show you're missing. It's not going to last forever, you know. You can sit on my stomach to watch it if you like. Oh, I'm so happy." At Café Rafaella I return from the bathroom to find him making silly faces and thumbing his ears at a baby across the room for as long as she's willing to watch him. He can't get enough of the rosebushes in the public garden behind the Jefferson Library or the orchids in the greenhouses of the Brooklyn Botanic Garden, where Judith takes him by subway.

As for me, with Judith enabling me to write again and Scott no longer in mortal danger, my anxiety is at bay. If I sometimes feel frustrated, impatient, or dissatisfied, well, who doesn't? Come May, when Judith graduates, I may be miserable again, but at least for now I'm fairly content—as, in his way, is he. When I ask him why, he says, "That's simple. It's because you stick by me, even though I'm such a dummy." And "Because I get so much face time with you."

We stroll through the neighborhood holding hands—as much out of affection as to maneuver through traffic. Down on Bleecker Street we stop in Rocco's Pastry Shop for decaf cap-

puccinos and order a baba au rhum and a plate of mini chocolate cannoli to split. Who cares if it's the middle of a Monday
afternoon? Once, I would have despised such indulgence as a
violation of discipline, but since I can't write after 2:00 p.m.
and I know our days are numbered, we do as we please. As we
blissfully scrape the last drops of foam from our cappuccinos
and lick the last of the cannoli cream off our forks, we work
ourselves up into a fine septuagenarian rapture, gazing tenderly
into each other's eyes to proclaim our love. To escape the
tyranny of the present imposed by his impairment, we indulge
in the pleasures of remembering: that over the years we con-
cluded our Bleecker Street shopping expeditions with a cappuccino here at Rocco's and a pound of chocolate meringues
to go; that here is where we ordered our wedding cake ("Really?" he asks, lighting up. "It came from here?" "Yes," I say,
pointing out the same cake in the display case). And after we
leave, as we traverse the blocks toward home, we revisit other
scenes of our past. Here, the restaurant where we had our first
dinner; there, the pocket park we call Bundle Square, after that
homeless man who yelled to Scott, "Watch out, she's gonna
cost you a bundle!"; there, the top-floor apartment in which
Ann gave us her blessing—all events he's able to recall, unlike
those that happened yesterday. Is his unrestrained delight a
function of his cognitive deficits or an overflow of love? I'll go
for love: given the options, why not *amor fati* and enjoy what's
left? As I first discovered in that hospital in Hawaii more than a
dozen years ago, in the scales of fulfillment, devotion may out-
weigh independence.

Should I be tempted to doubt this, I have only to remember
the heart-stopping panic I felt that time I lost him in Union
Square and found him hours later in the hospital all banged up,
or even just last month when he got away from Judith not once
but twice—once on the subway when the train doors closed

on him as he was trying to follow her off and somehow (but how? we'll never know) wound up at a police station on West 183rd Street; the other time at the Metropolitan Museum of Art, which he used to call his "temple" before he fell. While Judith and I frantically called the police, he managed to find his way home by taxi, unaware that he'd gone missing. Either he stiffed the driver or was the beneficiary of his charity, since the folded twenty-dollar bill I keep tucked inside his wallet for emergencies was still there, forgotten and untouched, and New York taxis didn't then take credit cards. Even though I'd been wild with anxiety, once I knew he was safe, I actually felt proud of him for making it home.

This man, who can no longer be counted on to find his way to our building from across the street, once had the equivalent of perfect pitch when it came to directions. He had such an unerring internal compass that even from deep inside an unfamiliar building he always knew which direction he was facing. In strange cities, whether on foot or by car, he mastered the map in moments; upon emerging from a building or entering an intersection he would know exactly which way to turn. "How do you know it's that way?" I'd ask. "I just know," he'd answer, and was invariably right.

Only once before the accident did I ever see him lose his way. It was in Colorado, in the late autumn of 1985, soon after our long romance had got its second wind. We had been hiking for hours in the mountains, where the aspens had turned a rich, shimmering gold, when we got so completely absorbed in each other that we wandered off the trail. In the mountains, knowing which direction you're facing at any moment won't help you find your way, because most of the trails are switchbacks, changing direction every few minutes. After an hour or two of searching for the trail that would take us down to where we'd parked the car, with the sun already setting behind the peak, he said reluctantly, "I don't want to alarm you, but I'm afraid if we don't find it soon, we may have to spend the night out here. Which won't be fun."

It sounded like fun to me until he listed the dangers— namely, that without flashlights, blankets, or extra water we could freeze, become dehydrated, and die of exposure. ("Plus bears!" adds Scott when I read him this scene.) I remember saying that I couldn't think of a better way to go, setting us off on a long set of riffs, with recurring spasms of laughter, on how, if we had to die, at least we'd die together and in the perfect place for it, on a glorious mountaintop amid the aspens and mountain sheep (of which we'd seen several that day)—when the trail we'd been seeking suddenly appeared before us, and in fifteen minutes we were back in the parking lot.

"The right ending," writes the novelist Michael Ondaatje, "is an open door you can't see too far out of." Whenever I try to imagine our story through Scott's eyes, I draw a blank—or at best a projection of my own story. Even before his fall he was a private person whose inner thoughts I could seldom guess. How much less can I know now that his mind is usually inaccessible even to himself. If he attempts to enlighten me, he often gets it wrong. Lacking understanding of what happened to him, he makes it up. *What accident?* he'll ask when I remind him, and propose a trip to China.

But can I claim to understand what truly happened either? *The unfathomable mysteries of the brain.* In his version, he's just getting old; in my version, he's gradually getting better. Neither is completely true, but we each cling to what we must believe, feel whatever it is we feel, see what it suits us to see, depending on the circumstances, the time, our mood, our need. I too, in a sense, keep making up our story moment by moment, out of hope, despair, anguish, optimism—and love.

Love, according to Wittgenstein, is not a feeling, like pain.
"Love is put to the test, pain not. One does not say: 'That was
not true pain or it would not have gone off so quickly,' " as one
may say of love. *Love is not love which alters when it alteration finds.*
Love put to the test survives. *For better and for worse. Till death do
us part.*

We're making the bed together, as we do every morning, when
suddenly, as he fluffs the pillows, Scott starts singing "Put the
Blame on Mame."

Last night for two hours we watched Rita Hayworth vamp
across the screen as Gilda on Turner Classic Movies, and though
he has no recollection of seeing *Gilda*—or any other movie
since his injury—the song he's belting out is Gilda's signature
number.

> Put the blame on Mame, boys
> Put the blame on Mame.

I'm stunned and thrilled at this latest triumph of memory.
Maybe it's because music is stored in a different part of the
brain than events or narratives, or perhaps he remembers the
song from long ago. Still, I rush around the bed and hug him
hard.

Later, at dinnertime, when I can't find the spatula in the
drawer where it belongs and ask him if he knows where it
could be, he says, "That's it, blame me. Everything's my fault.
But for a change, why don't you try putting the blame on
Mame?"

Not only has he remembered the song but he has added it
to his arsenal as surely as Gilda added it to hers. And though
I know Sarah would shake her head and accuse me of denial, I
want to leap up and celebrate.

"You see? I told you he's getting better," I tell Sarah excitedly on the phone. "And another thing. He remembers that we're going to visit you in January. He keeps asking if we shouldn't start packing."

"For a flight a month from now?"

"I know. His sense of time is gone, but at least he remembers that we're going. Isn't that remarkable?" Then I confide, "I take these latest feats of recall to be a sign of our incredible luck, the same luck that got me my book contract and sent me Judith just when I most needed them."

"Your incredible *luck*?"

Hearing her dubious opinion of my luck, I can practically see the scornful look on her face. So I quickly add, "Of course, I'm not counting the bad parts."

Sarah guffaws, then bursts out laughing. I pick up on her point. And soon we are drowning in laughter, gasping for breath.

"Not counting the bad parts," she repeats, coming up for air. "That's priceless. That's perfect. That's so you."

I can't but agree with her. The fact is, even the prospect of a nursing home, which was long my greatest bugaboo, no longer completely spooks me, not since Sarah pointed out that on the very day George or Scott is admitted, the women residents will start lining up for him.

When I tell Scott this thought, so comforting to me, he takes my hand and, with an impish gleam in his azure eyes, peers with me through the open door.

NOTES

2: THE HOSPITAL
46 **One night, reading about traumatic brain injury:**
www.biausa.org/Pages/types_of_brain_injury.html.

5: THRILLER
104 **Just as I'm teetering:** Nancy L. Mace and Peter V. Ru-
bins, *The 36-Hour Day*, first revised and updated edition
(New York: Warner Books, 2001).

6: COULD HAPPEN
125 **"Once brain-injured":** Dr. Yehuda Ben-Yishay of New
York University School of Medicine, quoted in Anemona
Hartocollis, "A Central Park Victim Recalls 'When I Was
Hurt,' and Her Healing," *The New York Times*, June 8, 2006.

7: TRAVELING ON
136 **I tell her about several new books:** Darrin M. McMa-
hon, *Happiness: A History* (New York: Atlantic Monthly
Press, 2006); Daniel Gilbert, *Stumbling on Happiness* (New

York: Knopf, 2006); Jonathan Haidt, *The Happiness Hypothesis* (New York: Basic Books, 2006). Since that conversation, Jennifer Michael Hecht's *The Happiness Myth* (Harper SanFrancisco, 2007) has also been published.

8: NUBBLE

161 **But now I read that sundowning:** www.alzla.org/ dementia/sundowning.html.

9: *AMOR FATI*

165 **"*Amor fati*," he said:** Friedrich Nietzsche, *Ecce Homo*, "Why I Am So Clever," section 10.

175 **"The right ending":** Michael Ondaatje, *Coming Through Slaughter*, quoted by Pico Iyer in *The New York Review of Books*, June 28, 2007, p. 40.

176 **"Love is put to the test":** Ludwig Wittgenstein, *Zettel* (Slips of Paper), ed. by G.E.M. Anscombe and G. H. von Wright (Oxford: Blackwell, 1967).